The 'Blue Squadrons'

The Spanish in the Luftwaffe, 1941–1944

Juan Arráez Cerdá & Eduardo Manuel Gil Martínez

Helion & Company

Helion & Company Limited
Unit 8 Amherst Business Centre
Budbrooke Road
Warwick
CV34 5WE
England
Tel. 01926 499 619
Email: info@helion.co.uk
Website: www.helion.co.uk
Twitter: @helionbooks
Visit our blog at blog.helion.co.uk

Published by Helion & Company 2023
Designed and typeset by Mach 3 Solutions (www.mach3solutions.co.uk)
Cover designed by Paul Hewitt, Battlefield Design (www.battlefield-design.co.uk)

ISBN 978-1-804512-39-5

British Library Cataloguing-in-Publication Data.
A catalogue record for this book is available from the British Library.

To Solete, my life.
To my parents, Salud and Eduardo.
To Caco and June.
To Merce and Ricardo.
To my grandparents Mercedes, Salud, Mami, Manuel and Juan.

To my old and admired friend, Lieutenant General Rafael Sánchez Ortega, in the hope that this book will help you to learn more about an important page in the history of our beloved Air Force.

Contents

Acknowledgements

Marisol García Gómez, Ricardo Ramallo Gil, Claes Sundin, José Fernández and Teodor Liviu Morosanu.

All pictures, except when noted, are from the archive of Juan Arráez Cerdá (member of the Advisory Council of the Air Force Historical Service).

Profiles by are Claes Sundin, José Fernández (Artipresse editor) and Teodor Liviu Morosanu.

List of Abbreviations

CASA – *Construcciones Aeronáuticas SA*
EdA – *Ejército del Aire* (Spanish Air Force)
GCE – *Guerra Civil Española* (Spanish Civil War)
HQ – headquarters
JG – *Jagdgeschwader* (fighter wing)
KIA – killed in action
LG – *Lehrgeschwader* (training wing)
MIA – missing in action
NCO – non-commissioned officer
OKL – *Oberkommando der Luftwaffe* (German Air Force High Command)
OKW – *Oberkommando der Wehrmacht* (German High Command)
USSR – Union of Soviet Socialist Republics
VVS – *Voenno-Vozdushnye Sily* (Soviet Air Forces)

Preface

After the Spanish Civil War, the winning side, commanded by General Franco, was evidently Germanophile thanks to the aid given by both Germany and Italy in the Spanish conflict, so when the news that the Third Reich had launched an attack against the Union of Soviet Socialist Republics (USSR) reached Spain on 22 June 1941, it was received with great satisfaction. In particular, the reaction was positive both because Spain had just emerged from a civil war in which it had defeated the communism that the USSR had tried to help impose and because the danger of a German invasion of Spain seemed to be receding, given the strained relations that existed in those days and the failure of the Hendaye negotiations in which Spain was asked to enter the war on Germany's side. The government therefore saw reason to ingratiate itself with Adolf Hitler.

That same day, General Francisco Franco, head of the Spanish state, offered to send a volunteer unit to fight on the Eastern Front alongside the German Army, an offer that was accepted by the German government two days later. The formation of the Blue Division (*División Azul*) was already underway.

But the Spanish Air Force and especially many Spanish pilots also wished to participate in the fight against the USSR and soon began preparations to organise a series of several successive expeditionary squadrons that would operate on the front for six months each. They became popularly known as the 'Blue Squadrons' (*Escuadrillas Azules*).

The initial desire was for each of the Blue Squadrons to provide air support to their Blue Division compatriots fighting in northern USSR, although this never came to fruition since the unit remained in central Russia despite requests from the Spanish government for its attachment to the Blue Division.[1] This decision was made at the last minute, as the initial Blue Division location was also in the central sector, which caused some consternation among the volunteers. The expeditionary squadron was supposed to be the equivalent of a *Luftwaffe Staffel*, although this was not the case in reality.

Apart from an emotional explanation (i.e., the return to combat against communism as had been done in the Spanish Civil War, or *Guerra Civil Española* (GCE), but now returning the visit to the Soviets), the Blue Squadron was born due to different interests that the Spanish government had in mind: on the one hand, a political explanation and, on the other, a practical and learning explanation.

The political explanation was that the creation of the Blue Squadron was a way of repaying Germany for the support it had given to the National Army through the Condor Legion during the years of the GCE.

During the GCE, the National Aviation (*Aviación Nacional*) had learnt a lot from its Italian and especially German comrades. One of the aspects that were assimilated by the newly created Air Force (*Ejército del Aire* (EdA)) and imposed on its Blue Squadron was that of pilot rotation. The pilots of the Condor Legion were rotated with the intention that the maximum number of pilots could take part in the GCE and thus accelerate their learning and handling of their modern aircraft.[2] The Spanish expeditionary squadron acted the same way during its participation in the Second World War in the *Luftwaffe*. Thanks to the Spanish pilots who spent months in combat in the USSR, the EdA was able to count on a large number of expert pilots who, in many cases, would reach important positions in both military and civil aviation. One of them even became Air Minister, Mariano Cuadra Medina (head of the 4th Squadron).

For these reasons, we should not really speak of the Blue Squadron but instead of the Blue Squadrons, as there were five Spanish squadrons that fought in Russian skies during their stay on the Eastern Front between September 1941 and March 1944. Approximately every six months, one squadron was relieved by the next.

1 The only link between the two Spanish units was a Ju 52 liaison owned by the Spanish airline Iberia.

2 Raúl Arias Ramos, *Legión Cóndor: Su historia 60 años después* (Madrid: Almena, 2000), p.18.

General Employment of the Squadrons in the *Luftwaffe*

As a unit roughly the size of a *Staffel*, the squadrons were assigned throughout their tour of duty to the *Luftwaffe*'s *Jagdgeschwader* 27 and 51, or JG 27 and 51. A German *Staffel* initially consisted of nine aircraft commanded by one officer. After the first months of the war, the number of aircraft assigned to each *Staffel* rose to 12–20 aircraft. Three or four *Staffeln* formed a *Gruppe*, and three or four *Gruppen* formed a *Jagdgeschwader* (fighter wing). The number of pilots varied from 20 to 25, ground personnel between 80 and 150, so each *Gruppe* consisted of about 40 to 50 aircraft and about 500 men. The pilots also performed secondary tasks on the ground, such as supervising aircraft maintenance and communication.

The five squadrons operated in the USSR without any relation to their Blue Division comrades, as their actions took place in the sector of Army Group Centre during such important moments like the German offensive on Moscow and the Battles of Kharkov, Smolensk and Kursk.

As with the Blue Division, there was no shortage of volunteers eager to form the Blue Squadron and 'pay the Soviets a visit back'. As is reasonable to expect, unlike the Blue Division, the Blue Squadron volunteers were all members of the EdA. These pilots were generally just as well trained as their German comrades.[1] This was because many of the Spanish pilots had flown with their German comrades in the Condor Legion in 1936–1939 and, therefore, had flown similar aircraft on many occasions and knew and mastered German tactics.

The practical and learning explanation for the creation of the Blue Squadron was to gather as much knowledge and training as possible while being part of the mighty *Luftwaffe*. In this way, all this information could be used to improve the performance of the EdA. This fact was the real reason why the pilots and expeditionary personnel were relieved after six months at the front. After all, the Blue Squadron copied the mode of operation of the Condor Legion during the GCE.

The missions carried out by the Spanish squadrons in Russia were generally of four different types:

- Free fighter missions (*Freie Jagd*): these were the most suitable missions for fighter pilots, as well as the most desired. Many victories were achieved with this type of mission.
- Ground attack missions: these were to damage enemy ground forces as much as possible. The pilots of the 1st Squadron took part in numerous missions of this type, although this was not the norm because they belonged to a fighter unit. Many of the Spanish pilots who took part in the GCE had flown missions of this type and were able to carry them out successfully.
- Escort missions: in these missions, the aircraft had to provide protection for formations of bombers, attack aircraft or reconnaissance aircraft. In many cases, these missions had the added difficulty of the slower speed of escorted aircraft compared to fighters. They required a strict control of the flying formations and to be very alert to the appearance of enemy aircraft.
- Alert or alarm missions: these consisted of always having two aircraft with their pilots in the cockpit ready to take off. On one occasion, there were four aircraft on alert. These aircraft had to be ready for most of the daylight hours, varying according to light and weather conditions.

1 A very important differentiating element was that, while the *Luftwaffe* pilots flew modern aircraft, the *EdA* pilots flew aircraft that were largely obsolete in 1941 Europe.

1

1st Squadron

Once Commander Ángel Salas Larrazábal, one of the best fighter pilots during the GCE, was appointed head of the unit, he began to appoint, from among the volunteer pilots, those who would make up the 1st Expeditionary Squadron, although Commander José Muñoz Jiménez, appointed to command the next squadron, managed to be added to it thanks to his friendship with Salas and his insistence to the Air Minister. Under his command, he had 16 pilots (the 15 pilots of the squadron and Major Muñoz) and 78 officers, non-commissioned officers (NCOs) and mechanical and service soldiers, bringing the total number of men to 125. The ground echelon was commanded by Major Ramón Salas Larrazábal, brother of the 1st Squadron's commander.

As noted, Commander Ángel Salas Larrazábal was a very expert pilot. He commanded the 2nd Squadron of the Morato Group in the GCE, during which he participated in 618 missions and 49 air combats, achieved 17 aircraft shoot-downs and 48 vehicles destroyed on the ground and was shot down on four occasions. He was the perfect leader for the 1st Blue Squadron, who would later pass on all the knowledge he learnt in combat to the Spanish EdA.

The members of the 1st Blue Squadron posing in the German uniform. Wearing a cap and with a dog on his left is Commander Ángel Salas Larrazabal.

Commander José Muñoz '*El Corto*' poses with a smile in front of several squadron aircraft. A pilot of small stature, but of great courage.

On 14 July, the squadron was formed and, 10 days later (July 24), left Madrid for Berlin. The journey to their destination was by train and took three days. They left *Estación del Norte* (North Station) and made stops at San Sebastián, Irún and Hendaye. Once in France, they were received with great honours. However, when the Spaniards left Hendaye for Paris, they were supposedly ordered to return to Hendaye to be disinfected against exanthematous typhus, as the French were suspicious of the state of health of anyone coming from Spain. They arrived in Berlin three days after leaving Madrid (27 July) and were received by the Spanish ambassador, Aeronautical Attaché Commander José Pazó and *Oberstleutnant* von Houwald, head of Fighter Pilot School No.1 (*Jagdfliegerschule* 1), located at the Werneuchen airfield, 28km from Berlin.

Ángel Salas Larrazábal, commander of the 1st Blue Squadron. He managed to shoot down six enemy aircraft and destroy another two on the ground.

Upon arrival at Werneuchen, they were greeted by a brass band playing the Spanish anthem. However, it was the anthem of the Spanish Republic, which had been defeated in the GCE, and this gave rise to some unease among the Spaniards. On 29 July, the pilots were informed of the training plan to be followed, and, that afternoon, they began training with Messerschmitt Bf 109 D and E aircraft.

Most of the Spanish pilots had flown the Fiat CR.32 during the last civil war, although some had already flown the Bf 109, Bf 109 B and Bf 109 E. For this reason, Major Salas divided his pilots into three groups: the first was made up of pilots already familiar with the Bf 109, the second was of those who had flown the 109 but had not done so for some time and would therefore fly the Arado Ar 96 first, and the third would carry out a somewhat more extensive programme. The days passed tediously, and the Spanish wanted to start their combat actions as quickly as possible, but the German organisation was slower.

The German bureaucrats regarded the Spaniards as novices who had never seen a modern aircraft, which caused a great deal of unease. It is worth mentioning an anecdote of Lieutenant Mechanic Fernando Urtasun, who, when he was being subjected to a knowledge test, used up the time he had until the last second to find three defects in an engine and

The pilots of the squadron at Werneuchen, still wearing EdA uniforms. In the centre, Major Muñoz stands out with his short stature.

Captain Aristides García López-Rengel smiling in the cockpit of his Bf 109 E-3 after a victorious mission. He would be missing in action shortly afterwards.

Two old friends from the GCE meet again: Major José Muñoz Jiménez and the well-known *Oberstleutnant* Werner Mölders.

then replied imperturbably, 'these are the three defects I had to see, and these other two I did not have to see, because you did not know they existed'.[1]

Spanish irritation was growing at what they considered to be too long a period of training, as half of them had overcome five area victories during the GCE and, between them, they had totalled 79 shootdowns.

GCE Shootdowns of the 1st Blue Squadron Pilots

Rank	Pilot	Shootdowns
Major	Ángel Salas Larrazábal	16 1/3
Major	José Muñoz Jiménez	–
Captain	Arístides García López Rengel	17
Captain	Javier Allende Isasi	7
Captain	Carlos Bayo Alessandri	11
Lieutenant	Alfonso Rubial Sabio	1
Lieutenant	Luis Alcocer Moreno Abella	5
Lieutenant	Esteban Ibarreche Arriago	7

Another photograph of *Oberstleutnant* Werner Mölders, this time saluting Major Salas in the presence of Major Muñoz and Lieutenant Busquets.

On 16 August, they took the oath of allegiance at the Werneuchen camp. Like their comrades in the Blue Division, the men of the Blue Squadron swore the usual oath used by the Germans but specified that it was only 'in the fight against communism'. It is important to emphasise that the Spaniards who fought against the USSR were generally fighting against communism and that this oath did not mean that they shared Nazi ideology with their German comrades (nor were the Spaniards generally Nazi in ideology, nor were all German soldiers Nazis).

It was shortly afterwards, during training, that Major Salas was informed that the Spanish squadron was not going to primarily act as a fighter squadron but rather as a ground attack squadron. The reason was the *Wehrmacht*'s need for *Luftwaffe* support in the attack against the vastness of the USSR.

Curiously, all the pilots of the 1st Blue Squadron were officers. In the *Luftwaffe*, it was unusual to see a captain in command of a *Schwarm* and more common to see him instead command the whole squadron or even a *Gruppe*.[2]

On 5 September, the 1st Squadron received its first combat aircraft: 12 Messerschmitt Bf 109 E-7/Bs, called '*Tripalas*' (Three Blades) by the Spaniards.[3] During the GCE, this aircraft model was already used in Spain and was fast and manoeuvrable (and therefore much appreciated by its pilots). Finally, having completed its training period, the 1st Squadron was ready to be sent to the front with its aircraft ready for take-off.

The ground crews (ground echelon) left on 22 September for their destination on the Eastern Front. On 26 September, the pilots took off with their planes to their destination, making two stopovers. The first was an airfield in Minsk, but only 11 aircraft landed there, as the Bf 109 flown by Major Muñoz had to make a forced landing, which caused minor damage to the aircraft. Although the idea was to stay in Minsk for a week, on 30 September, seven of the squadron's aircraft took off for their second stopover, specifically to finally land at the airfield from where they would begin their missions: Moschna, north-west of Smolensk. The other four aircraft remained in Minsk to be checked.

1 Juan Arráez Cerdá, 'Les Espagnols de la Luftwaffe: Les Escadrilles Bleues', *Ciel de Guerre*, 18 (2010), p.25.
2 Carlos Caballero and Santiago Guillén, *Escuadrillas azules en Rusia: Historia y uniformes* (Madrid: Almena, 1999), pp.18–20.
3 During the training period, rumours in Werneuchen said that the new F model might be the one the Spaniards would use, but this was not the case.

The cold and harsh climate of the USSR in 1941 did not prevent the Spaniards from fulfilling their mission. In this picture, Major Muñoz (on the left) poses with four comrades from the unit.

The Moschna airfield was a typical airfield of the time, as it had no facilities and the runway was the field itself. *Luftwaffe* personnel had to seek shelter in huts, often shared with peasants, and this was also the case for those men who wore the German uniform with a Spanish emblem on the right shoulder.

The pilots of the 1st Squadron taking the Oath of Allegiance to the *Führer* for combat on the Eastern Front.

The Spanish squadron was incorporated as '*15. Spanische Staffel*' into JG 27 of *VIII. Fliegerkorps*, *Luftflotte* 2. Its official designation was '15.(Span)/JG 27', and it was assigned to the command of Major Woldenga. Although belonging to the fighter JG 27, Blue Squadron operated as an autonomous unit within the ground attack group of *Lehrgeschwader* (Training Wing) 2, II(S)LG 2, which was under the command of Major Otto Weiss. 15.(Span)/JG 27 was structured into three patrols, with five aircraft each, and a staff (Spanish: *plana mayor*; German: *Stab*):

Staff: Commander-in-Chief Ángel Salas and Second-in-Command José Muñoz
1st Patrol: Captain Arístides García and Lieutenants Alfonso Ruibal, Ángel Mendoza, Ricardo Bartolomé and Abundio Cesteros
2nd Patrol: Captain Javier Allende and Lieutenants Luis Alcocer, José Lacour, Javier Busquets and Alfonso Gracia-Rodríguez
3rd Patrol: Captain Carlos Bayo and Lieutenants Esteban Ibarreche, Emilio O'Connor, Manuel Kindelán and Demetrio Zorita.

In front of a Bf 109 E, Lieutenants Ángel Mendoza and Esteban Ibarreche show a handkerchief by Elena Patiño (*Marquesa de Valparaíso y del Mérito*, 'Marchioness of Valparaíso and Merit'), with which all the pilots of the 1st Squadron were presented. It displays the coat of arms of the Blue Patrol during the GCE.

As we can see, all the Spanish pilots were officers, a fact that attracted the attention of their *Luftwaffe* colleagues.

The Blue Squadron used an emblem on its aircraft: a white circle with three birds in the centre (a falcon, a bustard and a blackbird), the phrase '*Vista, suerte, y al toro*' ('Sight, luck, and the bull', the motto of Joaquín García Morato's squadron during the GCE, which came from the world of bullfighting) and the number II (in Roman numerals).

At this time, the German Army was preparing its final blow against the city of Moscow in the so-called 'Operation Typhoon' (*Taifun*), which began on 30 September 1941. This German attack had led to the formation of 'pockets' of Soviet resistance, such as the one between Smolensk and Viazma.

The first mission in which Spanish pilots took part was on 2 October, coinciding with the start of Operation Typhoon. The 23 individual sorties they flew on this day were to escort Henschel Hs 123s and Bf 109s that were carrying out ground attacks against Soviet troops in the Orel area. That same day, the 1st Squadron suffered its first casualty when, after finishing an escort mission of the Hs 123s, Salas, Ruibal, Alcocer and Allende entered into combat with a formation of 22 MiG-3s, several Polikarpov I-16s and several DB-3 bombers. Despite the clash between the Soviet and Spanish aircraft, there were no casualties in either formation. However, Lieutenant Alcocer became disoriented and ran out of fuel after flying for over an hour, and he tried to make an emergency landing, during which he pulled out his wheels and was killed by the collision with his aircraft's collimator (a rule for crash landings was to never deploy the wheels and to always remove the collimator).

Lieutenant Alcocer's body was taken to Werneuchen in a Ju 52 that, on the return trip to Moschna, also picked up Major Muñoz, who was still in Minsk due to the breakdown of his aircraft.

Luftwaffe air support for the offensive against Moscow was provided by 1,300 aircraft mainly belonging to *Generalfeldmarschall* Albert Kesselring's *Luftflotte* 2. The fighter units involved were JG 51 (four *Gruppen*), JG 27 (two *Gruppen* and the 1st Blue Squadron) and two fighter *Gruppen* each from JG 3 and JG 53.

On 3 October, the four aircraft that had been left in Minsk in damaged condition (piloted by Captain Bayo and Lieutenants O'Connor, Mendoza and Kindelán) and the troops of the ground echelon (who had left by train on 22 September) arrived in Moschna. That same day, the 1st Squadron flew six close air support and ground attack missions, in one of which Major Salas destroyed several trucks of a Soviet convoy. Major Weiss' first congratulations to the Spanish squadron were received by Major Salas. The Spanish pilots participated in attacks against ground targets in the Battle of Vyazma–Bryansk and later in support of the left side of the German advance against Moscow.

During the first sortie of the following day, Major Salas took off with Captain Arístides and Lieutenants Ibarreche, Mendoza, O'Connor and Kindelán. Very soon, they saw two Pe-2s, and Salas went after them since he was lower. He started firing at 150m with his machine guns and then closer with his 20mm cannons, seeing pieces of the aircraft jump with his second burst, managing to shoot it down on the third and then seeing the pilot parachute out. They headed for the field but, shortly afterwards, spotted a very familiar silhouette from the Spanish war: a Polikarpov I-16 *Rata*, which was about to attack an Hs 123. Salas dived for it, and, when it was about to fire, the Russian gave a half-ton so fast that it broke its right wing, causing it to crash. They then returned to the field with the joy of the pilots having seen their commander achieve the squadron's first two victories. The same day, several Soviet convoys were strafed on the ground.

Close-up of the historic emblem used by the aircraft of the 1st Squadron.

The following day (5 October), there was an alarm take-off that had no consequences. In the afternoon, General von Richthofen (who had been in the Condor Legion during the GCE) visited to decorate Major Salas with the Iron Cross 2nd Class.

On 6 October, the Spaniards observed five MiG-3s over Nataskino during another escort mission of the II(S)LG 2 ground attack aircraft known to the Spanish as *'Angelitos'* ('Little Angels', these were Hs 123s) from the Spanish wartime. Salas and his men approached from below without being seen and fired on the last one, shooting it down.

The advance of the *Wehrmacht* caused the front line to be very far from the Moschna base, so, on 7 October, eight aircraft of the 1st Squadron were transferred to the Bjeloj airfield (to the north and near Orel, which had just been conquered by the Germans). Once at their new airfield, two patrols were formed: Salas, Rubial, O'Connor and Kindelán in the first and Arístides, Mendoza, Busquets and Cesteros in the second. One of the eight aircraft was damaged upon landing. This airstrip was in even worse condition than the one at Moschna (the ground was very muddy), although the Spaniards were only there for four days, during which a new Bf 109 E, flown by Lieutenant Lacour, arrived on 10 October to replace the squadron's damaged one. In the three days that they were able to fly missions (bad weather prevented the planes from taking off on 9 October), the Spanish flew 62 flights north of the Wjasma pocket and over the Sytschevka sector but without shooting down enemy aircraft. The last day, Major Muñoz (who had suffered the squadron's first failure) joined them in a Ju 52 also flown by Spaniards (Lieutenant Bartolomé).

From the Bjeloj airfield, they moved to the Konaja airfield, which was only a cleared field in the vicinity of a forest and a village. Again, there was no infrastructure to accommodate the Spaniards, who, on 12 October, had to pitch their tents despite the bitter cold. The same day, six planes arrived in Konaja first; hours later, two more planes arrived (those of Mendoza and O'Connor were awaiting repairs). Two aircraft remained in Bjeloj for repairs, and pilots Kindelán and Ruibal flew in a Ju 52 to Warsaw to pick up two new Bf 109 E aircraft.

From their new base, the Spanish resumed their missions on 13 October. During a reconnaissance mission over the Kalinin enemy camp, four Spanish Bf 109s encountered three I-16s. Major Salas attacked one of them relentlessly and so aggressively that the Soviet pilot crashed to the ground. Later, in another encounter with several MiG-3s, Captain Bayo managed to land one of the enemies. The same day, a biplane was shot down by Lieutenant Ibarreche. In one day, three enemy planes had been shot down, making 13 October the most successful day for the Spanish up to that point.

The ground echelon's arrival in the USSR. The men had a long journey to their destination, the Moschna airfield.

Victories were beginning to be won against the retreating Soviets, as the town of Kalinin was occupied by the Germans a few hours later.

On 14 October, one of the most beautiful services that Major Salas remembered from his stay in Russia took place. During a free fighter mission, four Spanish Bf 109s (two pairs formed by Salas and Bayo, who were accompanied by Lacour and Busquets) spotted three DB-3s escorted by fighters bombing *Wehrmacht* troops and immediately attacked them. Salas shot down the right point after setting fire to an engine and then manoeuvred to get into position to fire on the left point, but, in the heat of combat, he failed to notice that Bayo was a very short distance away, firing on the enemy aircraft after having shot down the leader of the enemy formation. Bayo, upon seeing Salas' manoeuvre, gave a strong lever to avoid the collision, but it was too late, and his propeller broke part of the rudder of Salas' Bf 109 E. Despite everything, Salas managed to shoot down the DB-3 and return to his field without any major problems. The result of the day was the downing of the three Soviet planes (two by Salas and one by Bayo). The same day, in a Fieseler Fi 156 *Storch*, *Generalfeldmarschall* Kesselring, head of *Luftflotte* 2, appeared to congratulate the Spaniards on their successes. In 12 days of action, they had performed 211 war services and achieved eight victories despite belonging to an assault *Gruppe*, which made it more difficult to encounter the Soviet fighters.

On 15 October, bad weather prevented the Spanish from flying, and, the following day, they were ordered to move to the recently conquered Kalinin. The new airfield was located on the front line, and the rapid advance of the German troops had created a vacuum between the forward troops and the bulk of their forces. This meant that the Spanish base was very close to the front line.

Once the city and airfield of Kalinin were occupied, the first mission was to escort Ju 52s carrying part of the 1st Blue Squadron's ground echelon to Kalinin, which was to be the new airfield for the Spanish. On 16 October, the first seven Spanish aircraft arrived at their new airfield, followed shortly afterwards by two more. During their flight there, Bayo, Lacour and Cesteros fought two DB-3s, one of which was shot down by anti-aircraft fire while the other smoked away after being hit by Bayo, who, in turn, was hit four times.

A few days later, three more aircraft joined the squadron so that it was once again complete (although part of the ground echelon that had not been transferred in the Ju 52s was still on its way). This fact is important, as we have seen how, on many occasions during the several days of fighting in which the Spaniards had participated, they had to fight without the entire ground echelon and with the difficulties that this absence posed.

On 17 October, during a free fighter mission, Salas, Muñoz and Ibarreche discovered an airfield without aircraft and set about strafing its installations and the trucks there. They could not imagine that, at that very moment, their own

Shortly after arrival at Moschna, Major Angel Salas in the cockpit of his Bf 109 E is greeted by Captain Arístides García before a mission.

One of the most eagerly awaited moments at the front, the '*rancho*' (meal). Several men from the squadron's ground echelon queue up, waiting for their turn and supervised by an officer.

Lieutenant Ibarreche resting between two training flights at Werneuchen in August 1941. It is noteworthy that the pilot wears the Spanish EdA uniform.

airfield was being attacked by five Russian tanks, two of which managed to penetrate the field. This attack was stopped by the quick intervention of the Hs 123s and Bf 109s, which pushed them back after destroying one tank. This is a good example to demonstrate not only the proximity of the base to the front but also that the Soviet Air Forces (*Voenno-Vozdushnye Sily* (VVS)) carried out several attacks against the Spanish base.

On 18 October, the Russian raids intensified. In the first raid, four I-16s and a DB-3 strafed Salas and Lacour, who had just landed but, without thinking twice, put their engines into overdrive and took off to attack them. Salas attacked the DB-3, which escaped into the clouds, while Lacour pursued the *Ratas*, who defended themselves by doing the '*pescadilla*' ('whiting', a formation in which one plane is behind the other, rotating as if they were a wheel). When Salas landed again, he was staked by nine MiG-3s that, fortunately, did not manage to hit him. In the next service, Arístides and Carracito took off. Arístides managed to shoot down an I-16 that landed on his own lines, but, as there were no witnesses, it could not be accounted for. The activity was incessant, and so, in the third service, Bayo and Cesteros fought with four DB-3s that managed to escape, although one was shot down by anti-aircraft. In the next service, Bayo took off again, this time accompanied by Lacour, to intercept five DB-3s, one of which he managed to hit. On their way back, as they were about to land, they saw three more DB-3s at ground level, and Lacour managed to touch down one of them, which crashed just eight kilometres from the Kalinin field. Later, there were two alarms in which Ibarreche chased a Pe-2, but two German Bf 109 Fs shot it down before he could catch up, while Lacour managed to scare off three MiG-3s.

The proximity of the Soviets prompted Major Otto Weiss (the commander of II(S)LG 2), on Sunday, 19 October, to order a state of alert for pilots and ground echelon and to explain the situation to them: the Junkers Ju 52s, with spares, fuel and supplies, could not arrive because of the heavy and intense rain that was falling, the thaw was preventing the early arrival of *Wehrmacht* troops, who were not expected until the evening of the next day at the earliest, and finally, the 1st Armoured Division was at a standstill and in the middle of the road cut off by the Russians at Torshok.

From that moment on, and in the face of an imminent Soviet attack, they had to take charge of the defence of the airfield in an urban area near the railway line between Leningrad and Moscow. As suspected, the Soviet attack took place, although in a different area from where the Spaniards were, capturing part of Kalinin.

At about 14:00, the order was given to move out to the trenches, which had been quickly constructed. The next day, the Russians began their attack from the north-west, managing to take the part of the city on the left bank of the Volga. The following day, they took the Torshok road junction with the railway to Leningrad, managed to cross the river and penetrated the airfield with about 300 soldiers, who were repulsed although not driven off this side of the river. The night was terrible, with heavy machine-gun fire and a fierce artillery duel. Finally, the next morning, the enemy was defeated and fled across the Volga.

Lieutenant Lacour gets out of his plane with help from a mechanic after a mission. The large scarf around his neck to protect him from the cold can be seen.

The pilot salutes the photographer shortly before the aircraft takes off on another combat mission. The shield of the 1st Squadron can be seen above the engine.

On 21 October, two Spanish Bf 109s were destroyed on the ground after a Soviet attack, as they were very close to the Spanish base. The same day, there were two more air raids on the Spanish grouping. On 22 October, the weather improved considerably, and German reinforcements began to arrive, temporarily reestablishing the front line and securing it. In addition, the squadron received ammunition and fuel (brought in by Ju 52s as well as Heinkel He 111s), so it was once again ready to fly. The airlift was also used to bring back the many wounded. Finally, the situation was brought under control on the front line, as the Soviet troops who had crossed the Volga were completely wiped out and road traffic was restored to the rear.

Faced with the enemy's proximity, on 23 October, the Hs 123 biplanes punished the Soviets again and again with their ground attacks while the Blue Squadron aircraft escorted them. One of the Spaniards, Lieutenant Busquets (a connoisseur of the aircraft, which Spain also had), got to fly one of these biplanes and collaborated with his German comrades by being temporarily attached to that *Luftwaffe* unit.

The nonstop fighting of the Germans and Spaniards in this sector of the front, together with Major Weiss' efficient organisation of the defence, which prevented the Spanish base from being encircled, earned Weiss the decoration of the oak leaves for his Knight's Cross of the Iron Cross.

To stop the wave of enemy aircraft attacking the Kalinin airfield, the Spanish were ordered to attack the Soviet base at Klin. Having received information that the Russians took off from this airfield to bomb them, which was where many of these air attacks came from, the German Air Force High Command (*Oberkommando der Luftwaffe* (OKL)) ordered them to attack the base at low altitude in order to destroy as many planes as possible on the ground. As this was a 'moustache' service, the nine veterans of the squadron reserved it for themselves. First thing in the morning, Lieutenants Ibarreche, Lacour, Cesteros and Carracito took off for the Klin field. In the afternoon, Captain Arístides and Lieutenant Busquets took off. On both occasions, the men were joined by Captain Bayo and Commanders Salas and Muñoz.

During the first pass of the morning service, Ibarreche set fire to a MiG-3 on the ground. Salas and Muñoz attacked a biplane of unknown type in the air, which managed to land but, while taxiing, was strafed by Bayo and Lacour, who set fire to and destroyed it. In the second pass, Salas set fire to another MiG-3, and his comrades strafed two more. However, when they were about to make the third pass, 15 MiG-3s appeared, so they decided to take altitude and return, receiving intense anti-aircraft fire that hit Salas' plane twice, which managed to land happily. But Lieutenant Cesteros crashed upon landing, damaging his Bf 109 E Werk N.3791 and suffering a 12cm head wound that had him evacuated to a Berlin

Captains Carlos Bayo and Arístides García López-Rengel examine a 20mm MG FF cannon on one of their Bf 109 Es. On Captain Bayo's right sleeve is the coat of arms with the colours of the Spanish flag and the inscription '*ESPAÑA*' (SPAIN) at the top.

hospital. In the second attack, which took place in the afternoon, as the Spanish had expected, the Russian planes were in the air and could not surprise them on the ground.

II(S)LG 2 *Gruppe* was given a few days rest at the Dugvino airfield, but the Blue Squadron remained at Kalinin and was temporarily attached to JG 52, its orders being very clear: to destroy Klin's aircraft, carrying out all necessary services and fighting in the air in the event of encountering enemy fighters.

Consequently, on 27 October, Klin was attacked again at dawn (the pilots were Salas, Muñoz, Ibarreche and Carracito) but without great success. Only one train running on the Leningrad–Moscow line was strafed and damaged, although 10 MiG-3s were found in the air and another seven taking off. In the afternoon, the attack was repeated with five Bf 109s piloted by Salas, Muñoz, Bayo and the recently incorporated Rubial and Kindelán, with Captain Bayo destroying a MiG-3 that was taking off. According to Major Salas:

> At 12:45 we took off five aircraft with the mission of strafing the Klin airfield, some 70 km from our lines. On the same day we had done another service over the same field and two others on previous days. As the last one had encountered fighters in the air in far greater numbers than ours, it was planned that this service should be done in cooperation with a *Gruppe* of German Messerschmitt Bf-109Fs, which would be tasked to fight the enemy fighters in the air while we strafed. We took off at the agreed time, waiting for the ten Bf-109Fs that were to accompany us to show up. Seeing that they did not arrive, we headed for the enemy camp, believing that the German planes would have gone straight there (I later learnt that they had not been able to take off because of the state of their airfield). Once we reached the target, and despite the fact that there were Russian fighters in the air, we made the strafing run, which was quite effective, as there were a large number of MiG-3s very concentrated and ready to take off. In one of those that tried to take off, when it came under fire from Captain Bayo, the pilot threw himself to the ground in a 'wheelie'. We came under very concentrated anti-aircraft fire, which hit some aircraft, including that of Lieutenant Rubial, who, on leaving the pass, radioed me that his engine had stopped. He continued talking for some time, until he finally told me that he was a hundred metres up and to the left of the railway heading north-west towards Kalinin, his position was about 12 km south-east of Staubecken Lake, as he commented that he was seeing the DB-3 that I was shooting down at that moment. From that moment on he was not heard from again. We hoped that he had landed well and had managed, by hiding, to reach our lines, as had happened many times in similar cases. Although this time he encountered the difficulty of the great distance, this has not happened so far, unfortunately …[4]

Indeed, neither Lieutenant Alfonso Ruibal Sabio nor the Bf 109 E Werk N.1341 he was flying were ever heard from again. He was the second casualty of the 1st Squadron.

During all the fighting, the Blue Squadron had belonged to II(S)LG 2, although this unit was sent to the rear after the fighting for Kalinin. This meant that the Spaniards became dependent on JG 52, although their official designation remained '15.(Span)/JG 27'. In particular, they tried to destroy (with little success) several artillery batteries harassing the Germans in Kalinin. The situation was so critical on the front, which was only a few metres from the airfield that was continuously hammered by Soviet artillery, that finally, on 29 October, in view of the intense shelling that the Kalinin field was receiving, the order was received to evacuate all available aircraft to the Starica, or Staritza, field, which was done without delay. The last two were evacuated by Captain Bayo and Lieutenant Kindelán, while part of the ground echelon left in two Junkers Ju 52s and two vans. Shortly afterwards, the 23 remaining Spaniards were able to leave in another Ju 52, which had to make two consecutive flights to do so. The next day, General von Richthofen appeared at the Staritza field and awarded Major Salas the Iron Cross 1st Class.

During the previous battles, the squadron operated successively from Moschna, Bjeloj, Konaja, Kalinin and Staritza; it managed to shoot down 10 enemy aircraft but suffered the casualties of one pilot killed, one missing and a third wounded.

At their new base, bad weather and icing made it difficult to maintain and fly the aircraft. Such difficult weather only allowed flights on days three through five of the new month, and that was only after having to chop the ice formed on the wings of the planes. On the fourth day, Major Salas, accompanied by Lieutenant Ibarreche, took off at 07:45 for a free fighter mission. Flying 500m away, they saw three MiG-3s, which they attacked, and Salas managed to touch one of them, which escaped while smoking, but he did not see it crash. Behind Salas was another MiG-3 that managed to hit him 11 times and force him to land, which he did perfectly at Joropolez in his own zone. He returned to the airfield the following day.

After several days at Staritza, on 6 November, the squadron was ordered to move to Rusa (80km from Moscow) on 12 November to take part in the offensive against Moscow. Only six aircraft arrived at Rusa, as wear and tear and inadequate maintenance due to bad weather and continuous fighting had left the squadron with half of its aircraft, so the rest

4 Arráez Cerdá, 'Les Espagnols de la Luftwaffe', 18, p.18.

Souvenir photograph of a 1st Squadron mechanic sitting on the wing of one of the unit's aircraft.

of the pilots had to transfer aboard a Ju 52. Although the airstrip was better than the previous airfields, the accommodation for the men was still quite inadequate. At Rusa, they were reunited with their 'old friends' from the assault *Gruppe*.

The bad weather and the cold (up to minus 25 degrees Celsius) prevented further Spanish flights until 11 November, when the two planes that were in a state of alarm (i.e., with their pilots in the cockpit, ready to take off) had to intercept a formation of Ilyushin Il-2s that were attacking the Spanish base. Although with difficulty, Lieutenant Medrano managed to take off and shoot down one of the Il-2s, but, by mistake, he forgot to note down some of the numbers of the German Bf 109 Fs that had seen the combat and was thus unable to record his victory. The other aircraft on alert was unable to take off due to mechanical problems at the last moment.

On 13 November, when the temperature had just reached minus 22 degrees Celsius, attack missions were flown against Soviet airfields at Nekoliskoje and Jubiskoje but without any victories to add despite engaging in aerial combat against seven MiG-3s.

On 14 November, three Spanish aircraft flew an escort mission of twin-engine Bf 110s. That same day, the ground echelon finally arrived at the Russian base, and Spanish pilots flew in the vicinity of Moscow.

Meanwhile, on 15 November, the second phase of the *Wehrmacht*'s attack on Moscow began. North-east of Moscow, the Blue Squadron was supporting German troops against the Soviet 30th Army on the Kalinin front, covering the advance of tanks and infantry in the Volokolamsk sector.

In the following days, numerous missions were flown to coincide with the German attacks aimed at capturing Moscow, during which a Soviet Po-2 was destroyed on the ground by Major Salas while escorting several Hs 123s on 18 November. To increase the number of aircraft, on 17 November, two Spanish pilots (Captain Bayo and Lieutenant Busquets) flew to Warsaw in a Ju 52 to pick up two aircraft for the squadron.

On 20–22 November, the Spaniards were unable to fly due to heavy fog. At dusk on 23 November, German troops managed to conquer Kalinin. During the previous week, the *Luftwaffe* (and therefore the Blue Squadron) had to fly from airstrips very close to the front line and, at times, within firing range of Soviet artillery. On 25 November, the Blue Squadron received three Messerschmitts on loan from a German squadron.

The most fateful day for the 1st Squadron was 27 November. The morning services had gone well, but visibility was poor, and it was impossible to descend to 200m or 330m if they wanted to discover and hit the target. At 12:00, seven planes took off in two patrols. The first was led by Salas with the mission of protecting a *Gruppe* of Junkers Ju 87 B *Stukas*, which attacked the Moscow road 10–15km from Solnetschnogorsk. The second was of two planes piloted by Captain Arístides García López and Lieutenant Kindelán, who carried out the direct protection of four Hs 123s, which

One of the Spanish Messerschmitts, as can be seen by the emblem painted on the engine, being repaired for take-off on a new combat mission.

attacked about five kilometres north-east of Istra, and the Bf 109 E of Commander Muñoz, which was loaded with bombs to support the *Angelitos* and then rejoin Salas' patrol. The later General Kindelán recalled:

> I was flying with Captain Arístides to give protection to the '*Angelitos*' and Commander Muñoz's 'Messers'. When we arrived over the target they began to bomb, carrying out a chain attack; I saw how the commander's plane was also launched and how, when it was diving at an angle of about 30°, it was hit by an anti-aircraft impact and caught fire. I shouted: 'Commander, dive!' And about a hundred metres up I saw him throw the canopy and try to get out, but he was too low and the parachute did not open completely. I alerted Captain Arístides that I was separating to take a pass and see what had happened, but he did not answer me. When I came down all I could see was a Russian tank approaching the place where the plane had fallen and I fired a few shots at it. I went up and started calling Captain Arístides, but got no answer, so I joined the Hs 123s and went back to the field with them.[5]

At first, it was thought that Captain Arístides' absence was due to a mistake or bad weather and that he would have landed in a field on the German lines, but, as time went by, his disappearance had to be accepted.

In the afternoon of the same day, after a protective service, Major Salas took off to look for his friend Muñoz despite the heavy anti-aircraft reaction, which hit him once. With him went Lieutenants Lacour, O'Connor and Zorita. Lieutenant Kindelán, in a Fi 156 *Storch*, landed with the *Wehrmacht* unit that had witnessed the battle and confirmed Muñoz's fall behind Soviet lines. Nothing was heard of the fate of the Spanish pilot, and the squadron suffered a very important casualty, as he was one of the bravest and most skilled pilots in the whole National Aviation during the GCE.

On 28 November, saddened by the losses of their comrades, they moved to the Kalinin airfield, a good field with permanent facilities.[6] The eight available pilots flew the aircraft, which were later joined by one more brought by Lieutenant Bartolomé. Their first service from there was as free fighters in the Istra and Dimitrov sectors and almost cost the loss of Lieutenants Mendoza and Lacour, who, upon their return, got lost and made two emergency landings, with the landing gear inside, near the village of Medvedjkino, 200km from their airfield. They did not manage to return until 3 December.

Missions were carried out day after day on the vast Soviet front. For example, on 30 November, six free fighter missions were flown in pairs in the Dimitrov–Ignatova area (Moscow Canal). Anti-aircraft artillery riddled the *Luftwaffe* aircraft, making any mission difficult. In the first of the services, in the charge of Salas and Ibarreche, the commander was hit from the ground and noticed that his left steering control was broken, so he returned to the field and landed happily. However, in the taxiing, the right wheel broke, but Salas managed to avoid a wheelie thanks to his skill. For his part, Lieutenant Zorita spotted a light aircraft that was about to land and strafed it until it caught fire.

On 2 December, free fighter services were also carried out in pairs in the Dimitrov–Jakhroma–Oserezkoije–Alabuschenko sector, which passed without incident except the third, when Allende managed to hit a Russian plane, and the sixth, when Allende and Bartolomé fought against three MiG-3s but were unable to shoot down any of them. Every

5 Arráez Cerdá, 'Les Espagnols de la Luftwaffe', 18, p.18.
6 This airfield was the closest to Moscow of all those where any Spanish squadron had been.

Lieutenants Bartolomé, O'Connor, Carracido and Zorita during a moment of rest, posing on a 1st Squadron aircraft, where the unit's emblem is clearly visible.

day, all the pilots flew several missions, so exhaustion was beginning to show, but the German advance towards Moscow required a new effort from all the men.

Two days later, the 1st Squadron flew its last two war missions on the front. In the first, Allende, Ibarreche, O'Connor and Zorita fought three MiG-3s and five Pe-2s, without success. In the second, also a free fighter over the Moscow Canal, Lieutenants Mendoza, Bartolomé and Zorita were flying over the Fjudosuska–Jajroma sector when Mendoza (who commanded the formation) spotted several enemy aircraft and ordered his two points to dive-bomb them. As Mendoza carried out the manoeuvre, he could see how Bartolomé was climbing again while leaving a white trail that Mendoza assumed was condensation. Warning him by radio to not continue climbing and to follow him, he got no reply. Turning to the right, Mendoza saw a parachute and was certain that it was his comrade, whom he saw falling very close to the German lines. Unfortunately, the Soviet counterattack had already begun and prevented Bartolomé's rescue. Lieutenant Ricardo Bartolomé was never heard from again.

Lieutenant Demetrio Zorita poses proudly, smiling next to his Bf 109, painted with white brushstrokes to make it less visible.

In the afternoon of the same day, the temperature dropped again, reaching minus 35 degrees Celsius, and the aircraft engines refused to start.

But the tide of the war was beginning to turn, and the Soviets not only resisted the Germans but also began to launch attacks against them. On 5 December, in temperatures of minus 35 degrees Celsius, the German High Command (*Oberkommando der Wehrmacht* (OKW)) ordered a halt to the offensive against Moscow. Yet the battle in the sector continued, as the Russians counterattacked and Army Group Centre was forced to go into defensive positions. The Soviets managed to keep their aircraft in operation and began to harass the *Luftwaffe*, which found it very difficult to get the planes into action because of the cold. The Klin airfield was very close to the front line, which, together with the cold temperatures, led to the decision to move the Blue Squadron to safer positions. In addition, General Zhukov's major offensive began on 6 December along the entire Moscow front, opening a 10km gap in the Kalinin sector. The situation for the Germans and Spaniards changed drastically in just several days. A retreat to defensive positions was necessary.

The morning of 8 December dawned bitterly cold, but, fortunately, the temperature did not drop below the minus 38 degrees of the previous night. At about 09:00, the *pater*, as the chaplain is familiarly known in the Spanish Army, began Mass while waiting for a Ju 52 in which the Blue Squadron was to be transferred to the airfield at Rusa. But, shortly before the Mass ended, Major Salas was ordered to report to Major Wilhelm Lessmann, *Kommodore* of JG 52, who commanded the airfield and the air units based there and who reported that the critical situation there was being suffered because only JG 52 personnel and a 20mm battery were available. The Soviets were advancing towards Klin unopposed and were only minutes away from the German–Spanish base, so Major Lessmann organised the defence of the base with the Blue Squadron, *I. Gruppe* of JG 52 and an anti-aircraft battery. Immediately, the Spanish squadron ordered a German officer to prepare a platoon to take charge of blowing up the planes (the Blue Squadron had only four Bf 109s left in flying condition) if necessary and Major Salas to:

> First: order four of your pilots to take off with the four remaining aircraft in flight status and take them to the airfield at Rusa.
>
> Second: load as many spare parts as possible into two vans that, under the command of an officer, are to withdraw to the village of Nekrasino, where they will await orders. The rest of the material and equipment is to be abandoned.

Upon his return, Major Salas gave the corresponding orders, and then the trucks, fully loaded, left under the command of Lieutenant Ramón Salas. The rest of the squadron formed up and then marched towards the command post. Despite the Spanish attempt to evacuate, the speed of the Soviets caused the men of the Blue Squadron (together with their German comrades) to deploy in a defensive line in one area of the base. The Spanish force consisted of four platoons and command. For their part, an attempt was made to take off the four Bf 109s to evacuate them, but icing on the wings and windscreens prevented the flight (Captains Allende and Bayo and Lieutenants Ibarreche and Cesteros had managed to take off but were forced to land because of the icing on the wings), so the four pilots joined the Spanish defensive formation, which numbered 66 men in total. By nightfall, the situation was critical, and preparations were made to blow up the hangars if the Soviets approached the base.

Fortunately, at dawn on 9 December, the situation was not so difficult, although the base was attacked by the VVS (in charge of four DB-3s accompanied by six I-18s) without causing significant damage and under constant artillery fire. Attempts were made to get the four Spanish aircraft to take off, but, again, this proved impossible. A Ju 52 transport plane arrived at the base and began to evacuate some men (a brigade and five mechanic corporals bound for the Russian camp). By nightfall, there was heavy shooting around the airfield, and the danger was again at its height.

At dawn on 10 December, the situation was extremely dangerous at the airfield, as the Russian outposts were there. Major Lessmann reported that the situation had seriously deteriorated: the enemy was beginning to attack the airfield directly in an attempt to encircle it while no more of their own aircraft could land since the whole area was under rifle and machine-gun fire. Consequently, all the planes were ordered to take off immediately in order to try saving them once again. On the Spanish side, Captains Bayo and Allende and Lieutenants Ibarreche, Mendoza and Cesteros tried. Cesteros was unable to get off the ground and had to abandon the Messerschmitt in the middle of the field. Allende returned after 20 minutes due to an absolute lack of visibility and with several hits. Ten minutes later, Captain Bayo also returned after being hit in the engine. Ibarreche's capture, by mistake, was at Spaskoe, between Klin and Volokozomask, on his own lines. Only Lieutenant Mendoza managed to get there. None of the 10 Bf 109 Es of JG 52 made it.

Despite the entire field being pounded by rifle and machine-gun fire, a Ju 52 managed to land at about 12:00 and quickly took off again, taking with it Lieutenant Zoríta, who was ill, and a mechanical corporal. Two hours later, another Ju 52 also managed to land and evacuated some of the 1st Squadron's equipment, as well as the *pater* and six more men from the ground echelon. Some German troops who arrived in the area managed to ease the pressure that the Soviets were exerting on the airfield. Thanks to this brief respite, Major Lessmann ordered the repair of the aircraft still on the airfield in an attempt to evacuate them. He also gave the order for the men of the Blue Squadron to be ready for combat during the early hours of the morning. The Spaniards positioned themselves in a snow-covered defensive position but with little ammunition.

As we can see, the situation was very tense for several days and nights, during which the airfield was very close to being captured by the Soviets due to the lack of troops to defend it. Thanks to the pilots and men of the ground echelon of the Spanish squadron and the *Luftwaffe* unit with which they shared the airfield, who were 'converted' into infantrymen, it is possible that, at dawn on 12 December and given the total impossibility of resisting, the order was given to evacuate the airfield. At around 08:30, the Spaniards, under the command of Captain Allende, set off on foot towards the village of Nekrasino, 15km away. Meanwhile, Lieutenant Urtasun and several of his men were in charge of blowing up the hangar and the planes. Major Salas and Major Lessmann left several hours later by car and were the last to leave the airfield.

The march on foot was terrible for the Spaniards, as they were not used to walking quickly on snow-covered roads, and Lieutenant Urtasun, who later left the camp in a carriage, had to pick up several of the exhausted soldiers along the way.

Once in Nekrasino, they were housed in an empty house but had absolutely nothing to shelter them from the cold, as all their belongings had to be abandoned.

The next day, the march to Pavel'cevo was resumed, but the column was attacked by six Pe-2s and a little later by another three, one of which was shot down by German anti-aircraft. When they reached Petrovskoe, Captain Allende, with ulcerated feet, refused to continue despite Major Lessmann's insistence, for such was his stubbornness that, since the GCE, he had been known among his comrades as '*La Mula*' (The Mule). Left alone, he had the good fortune that, after several hours, a straggling German tank picked him up and brought him to the rear but not before he had been taken for a madman.

The next day, the column managed to board several trucks, but within a few minutes they were attacked by several I-16 *Ratas*, which fortunately did not cause any casualties. The journey continued, and, at 03:00 on 14 December, they managed to reach Rusa, where they rested for two days before setting off in several Junkers Ju 52s for the Dugvino airfield, where the squadron was to reorganise.

Once in Dugvino, the 1st Squadron met the sad end to which the OKL had brought it. The Spaniards should never have been used as a 'sacrifice squadron' since all of them were expert fighters (as previously noted, between all the pilots, they had dozens of aerial victories in the GCE), not infantrymen. Moreover, the purely fighter German squadrons never operated from the forward airfields that would force them, as had happened with the Spanish squadron, to destroy their own aircraft. With the successive Blue Squadrons, the *Luftwaffe* would not make the same mistake.

In the days that followed, the Spaniards became increasingly restless because of the absolute lack of news of the seven Spaniards who had been left behind for one reason or another, but, little by little, they arrived. Lieutenant Busquets arrived flying a Bf 109 E, which was interpreted as meaning that the OKL intended to completely re-equip the squadron. At Dugvino, the Spaniards had the opportunity to meet the German Ju 87 ace Hans Ulrich Rudel, who was there with his squadron. Faced with this situation, on 4 January 1942, the order was received to move to the Vitebsk camp, where the list of material needed for normal operation was drawn up and Lieutenants Urtasun and Hervás were sent to collect it.

When the 1st Squadron had already taken delivery of nine new Messerschmitt Bf 109 E aircraft, an order was received from *VIII. Fliegerkorps* informing them of their forthcoming repatriation to Spain and that they had to deliver aircraft and spare parts. However, despite this order and because of the Soviet harassment, the Spaniards did not neglect their defence and carried out some services to protect their airfield, right up to 5 February, when Lieutenants Ibarreche and Carracido carried out the last one.

Finally, on 11 February, the decorations were awarded to all the personnel of the 1st Squadron, with Commander Salas receiving the German Cross (*Deutsches Kreuz*) in Gold, the only Spanish pilot among all the Spanish squadrons to receive it.

The return to Spain then began, while, in Spain, the 2nd Blue Squadron was preparing to take over. On 17 February, the Spaniards of the Blue Squadron returned to Werneuchen, and, on 28 February, they were crossing the Spanish border. On 1 March, they arrived at Madrid's *Estación del Norte*, where they were greeted with great joy by a crowd of people. The day before, from the same *Estación del Norte*, the 2nd Blue Squadron had left for Germany. The 1st Blue Squadron was officially disbanded on 4 March 1942.

After approximately six months in combat, the 1st Squadron returned to Spain, leaving five pilots dead and one soldier in the USSR (Major Muñoz, Captain Arístides García López and Lieutenants Alcocer, Ruibal and Bartolomé – victims of Soviet anti-aircraft artillery or accidents). For its part, the 1st Squadron flew 422 combat missions, as bomber protection and free fighter, and took part in 94 air combats, managing to shoot down 10 confirmed enemy aircraft (six by Major Salas Larrazábal, two by Captain Bayo and one each by Lieutenants Lacour and Ibarreche), four probable shootdowns (one each by Commander Salas, Captains Bayo and García López and Lieutenant Mendoza) and to set fire to five aircraft on the ground (two by Commander Salas and one each by Lieutenants Cesteros, Zorita and Ibarreche). In addition to the shootdowns, numerous decorations were awarded to both pilots and men of the ground echelon during the months of combat.

Several Spanish mechanics follow the explanations of one of them on various aspects of the Bf 109 E.

The 1st Squadron experienced multiple airfield changes, bad weather and Soviet ground offensives that forced the men of the squadron to act as infantry. In addition, in many cases, the squadron pilots could not count on all the aircraft since, due to the repairs of the Bf 109s and the various base changes, many aircraft remained at the previous airfield awaiting repairs before being reintegrated into the squadron. Also, for the same reason, the ground echelon in many cases went on difficult marches across Soviet lands in search of their squadron. Nevertheless, despite lacking adequate infrastructure, available aircraft and even pilots (who had to make several trips to pick up new aircraft for the squadron), the Spanish aircraft had to be operational at all times.

The 1st Blue Squadron was regarded very positively by Germany due to its courageous performance on the Russian front. This widespread satisfaction can be seen in an article in the Andalusian edition of the *ABC* newspaper on Wednesday, 15 July 1942:

Several mechanics read the newspaper *PUEBLO*, which they had just received thanks to the Ju 52 liaison that the Spaniards had at their disposal on the Eastern Front.

Mechanics read a newspaper next to the engine of a Bf 109 E, showing the 1st Squadron's coat of arms.

> Berlin 14. The relief of the Spanish aviators who form the glorious Blue Squadron, provides an opportunity for the Berlin newspaper *Völkischer Beobachter*, to gloss, in a vibrant article, the heroic performance of this squadron in their fight against communism on the Russian Front.
>
> The newspaper, the organ of the German National Socialist Party, recalls the famous motto of the García Morato squadron: '*Vista, suerte, y al toro*'; under which the Blue Squadron also fights, and praises the 'ace' of the Spanish aviators, who after infinite feats during the crusade, saw his life cut short in an aviation accident, shortly after Franco's victory.
>
> 'The Blue Squadron was created when the Blue Division was organised, and under the command of Major Salas, it demonstrated its mastery of the air during the fighting last winter. The victories it achieved are testimony to the fact that the Blue Squadron retains the old fighting spirit of that of García Morato, and its casualties once again cement its fame.'
>
> 'Today', continues the *Völkischer Beobachter*, 'the second Blue Squadron is ready for combat. It is also composed of the best Spanish fighter aviators, and its leader, Commander Salvador, was victorious in 37 air battles, and is a survivor of the García Morato squadron.'
>
> 'Once again, these men are facing the Soviets, against whom they bravely risked their lives in defence of the freedom and culture of Europe, and they will continue the glorious tradition of García Morato's squadron. Good luck, says their motto, and we wish them good luck, once again.'[7]

Despite this, there were formal protests from the Spanish authorities (and the pilots themselves) that they had been primarily used as a ground attack unit, which caused more casualties than expected in the Spanish unit.

The brave behaviour of the Spaniards enabled them to receive many decorations. As noted, Major Salas received the German Cross after receiving the Iron Cross 2nd and 1st Class. Major Muñoz, Captains Allende and García López Rengel and Lieutenants Lacour, Ibarreche and Busquets received the Iron Cross 2nd and 1st Class. The Iron Cross 2nd Class was awarded to pilots O'Connor, García, Kindelán and Mendoza; mechanics Urtasun and Méndez and Corporal Álvarez also received it. The rest of the 1st Blue Squadron members were awarded the Cross of Military Merit with Swords.

7 Eduardo M. Gil Martínez, *Fuerza Aérea Española durante la 2ª Guerra Mundial* (Madrid: Almena, 2019), p.88.

DIARIO ILUSTRADO DE INFORMACION GENERAL. 25 CENTIMOS

ABC

DIARIO ILUSTR DO DE INFORM CION GENERA 25 CENTIMOS

FUNDADO EN 1905 POR D. TORCUATO LUCA DE TENA

LA ESCUADRILLA AZUL

Teniente O'Connor

Teniente Zorita

Teniente Ruibal

Teniente Ibarr

Teniente Kindelán

Teniente Bartolomé

Teniente Lacour

Teniente Alc

Teniente Mendoza

Teniente G. Carracido

Teniente Busquets

Teniente Cesteros

El domingo ha regresado a Madrid, después de su heroica actuación en Rusia, la escuadrilla española. He aquí a sus componentes, condecorados todos con la Cruz de Hierro. (Fotos Zegrí.)

Comandante Salas

Capitán Allende

Capitán Arístides

Capitán Bayo

Comandante Muñoz

Front page of the *ABC* newspaper of 3 March 1942, announcing the return of the 1st Squadron to Spain. These men were received as true heroes, which was not the case with the following Blue Squadrons.

Major Salas, Captain Bayo and Lieutenant Carracido with another lieutenant from the ground echelon during a chat. The thick woollen pullover worn by the commander to avoid the intense cold is remarkable.

Captain Arístides López García-Rengel of the 1st Blue Squadron smiling in the cockpit of his Bf 109 E. He would disappear in combat shortly afterwards.

The always busy mechanics of the 1st Squadron at work getting this Bf 109 E ready for flight. Their experience with the EdA's Messerschmitts greatly helped the very high performance of these men in the USSR.

The coat of arms of the Spanish troops on the Eastern Front, with the colours of the Spanish flag. Both the men of the Blue Division and the Blue Squadron carried it.

2

2nd Squadron

The 2nd Expeditionary Squadron should have had as its leader Major Muñoz, who had died in Russia while flying with the 1st Squadron. It was therefore necessary to choose a new commander, who was Major Julio Salvador Díaz-Benjumea. He was an officer of great prestige and the only survivor of the mythical Blue Patrol (*Patrulla Azul*), who had won 23 victories in the recently concluded GCE. The post he held before being assigned to the 2nd Blue Squadron was that of head of the Fighter School (*Escuela de Caza*) in Morón, so everything he had learnt in the Russian skies could be used to train the new Spanish pilots.

In the 2nd Squadron, some variations were introduced with respect to the rules of the 1st Squadron, which would also apply to the following squadrons. The first was that its commander-in-chief would be designated as 'inspector commander' while the direct command of the squadron would fall on the most senior captain, as this had the advantage of giving the commander-in-chief more freedom to carry out other functions apart from war services (e.g. administrative, diplomatic and, above all, learning everything that could be useful for implementation into the functioning of the EdA). The commander-in-chief had to resolve organic and administrative matters with his superiors in the *Luftwaffe*,

The banner of the 2nd Blue Squadron during their training period in Werneuchen, Germany.

Julio Salvador Díaz-Benjumea, commander of the 2nd Blue Squadron, chats with the commander of another *Luftwaffe* squadron. The badge with the Spanish flag is clearly visible on his right sleeve. His squadron managed to shoot down 19 enemy aircraft during his time in Russia.

and he did not want to end up like the case of Commander Ángel Salas, who was never absent from the airfield for a single moment nor failed to perform a single war service of those that corresponded to him as just another pilot.

The 2nd Expeditionary Squadron in Russia was formed on 6 February 1942 at Morón de la Frontera (headquarters (HQ) of the Fighter School), where they had a period of training until 2 March. The Tablada base near Seville was also used, where they arrived on 8 February. During the training, the pilots flew Messerschmitt Bf 109 Bs and Bf 109 Es to familiarise themselves with the aircraft that they would use in Russia (specifically, the Bf 109 B-2 '6-19' and the Bf 109 E-3 '6-110' and '6-115'), although CR.32s and Bücker *Jüngmanns* were also used. In general, their training can be considered to have been poor.

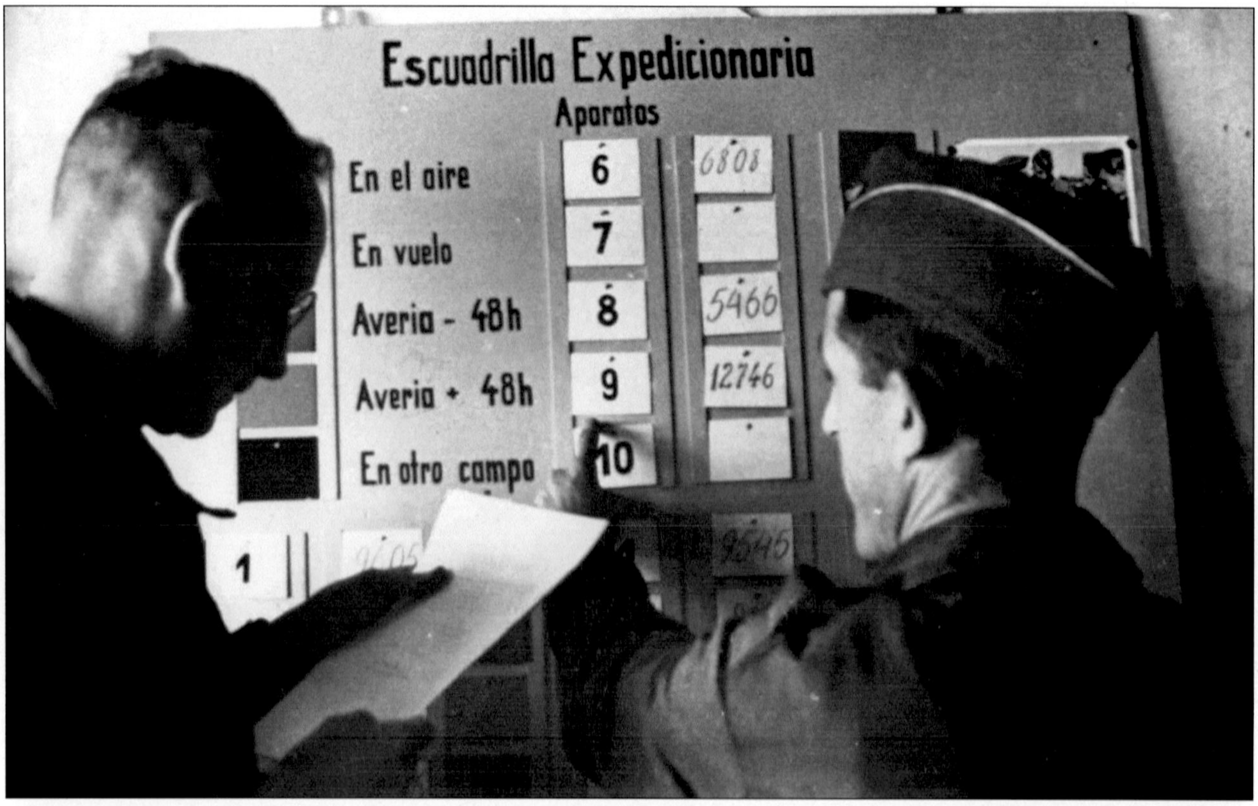

The operational status board of the squadron's aircraft. From top to bottom: aircraft flying, aircraft airworthy, aircraft under repair in less than 48 hours, aircraft under repair in more than 48 hours and aircraft at another airfield.

In addition, there was a Ju 52 owned by the airline Iberia (more modern and with better engines than those belonging to the EdA) that was painted in the *Luftwaffe* colours. Its mission was to liaise between the 250th Infantry Division, or Blue Division, which was fighting in the north of the USSR, and the Blue Squadron. It was also used to transport mail between the two units and the cities of Berlin and Madrid.

In this squadron, unlike the 1st Squadron, the pilots came from three different situations:

- Young pilots who had just received their pilot qualifications at the Fighter School
- GCE veteran pilots
- Officers who had participated in the GCE not as pilots but in other branches (e.g., cavalry or infantry) and who, after the end of the war in Spain, had completed the pilot course.

There were many applications to join the 2nd Squadron, but, in the end, only 15 pilots were chosen, along with the inspector commander and his second-in-command.

On 24 February, they left for Getafe Air Base, near Madrid, where they were visited by Air Minister General Juan Vigón, who gave them the order to leave for Germany on 28 February. On 1 March, they stopped in San Sebastián and then went on to France, where, upon arrival in Hendaye, apart from being welcomed, they had to undergo the pertinent medical examination, as had happened with the 1st Squadron. The journey then continued without further delay, passing through Bordeaux, Paris and Frankfurt to arrive at Werneuchen on 4 March at 09:30. After being distributed and billeted, the 2nd Squadron began its training the following day.

The initial instruction was not with the planes but completely theoretical (e.g., the state of the Eastern Front, cartography, handling of the Mauser 98K rifle, how to make emergency landings in Russia and silhouettes of Soviet planes),

The members of the 2nd Blue Squadron at the Werneuchen airfield in Berlin, where they trained, wearing the German uniform for the first time.

Several members of the 2nd Squadron ground echelon during weapons training. Of particular note are the helmets with the *Luftwaffe* eagle. The right side of the helmets are painted with the red–yellow–red shield with the Spanish flag.

which made the Spanish soldiers who wanted to start flying impatient. Faced with the Spanish complaints, the Germans made many incomprehensible excuses, but things went on as usual.

On 17 March, the Oath of Allegiance to the *Führer* for the Eastern Campaign was taken by the Spaniards, who for the first time wore the German uniform, as until then they had only used the Spanish uniform (which was the same as that used by the Germans, but on the upper part of the right shoulder was the national coat of arms in red, yellow and red with the word '*ESPAÑA*', 'SPAIN', above it). This was done with the presence of General Eduardo González Gallarza, visiting Germany with the purpose of obtaining new German aid for the Spanish aeronautical industry, such as the construction under patent of the Bf 109 or the He 111. The feeling of the Spanish officers was that they were being treated as conscripts and not as what they really were, but the strict German organisation did not allow for any other way of organising the squadron.

The Spanish pilots were finally able to fly on 23 March with two veteran Bf 109 Es, with which very few pilots actually flew, and only in a 10-minute flight with one take-off and two landings. The 'Emils' were not the same aircraft model that the 2nd Squadron would receive: the Messerschmitt Bf 109 F-2. On 25 April, the Spanish received the news that they would be flying the F model, which was received with great joy and expectation, although they were not able to do so until the second week of May. At the same time, they learnt that the squadron would be incorporated as *Staffel* 15 of JG 51 *Mölders*. This information was really important because, unlike the 1st Squadron, they would act as a true fighter squadron and not as an assault squadron. The Spaniards were tired of the countless theoretical lectures they were forced to attend and the few flights they made, as they only had four aircraft at their disposal. The time they had to stay in Werneuchen was also extended until the beginning of June due to the delay on the part of the *Luftwaffe* in delivering their 15 Bf 109 F-2s, which, following Spanish custom, were christened '*Zacutos*'.[1]

44: Thanks to the efforts and magnificent performance of the squadron's mechanics, the Spanish unit had aircraft ready for flight almost continuously.

1 These Bf 109 F-2s were aircraft that had been used by other *Luftwaffe* units and required an overhaul before being delivered to the Spaniards.

At the beginning, when they had only received five aircraft, two of them were soon out of service. On 12 May, during a session of 'take-offs and landings' that Lieutenant Federico Garret Rueda (better known by the nickname '*El Chanquete*') was carrying out, his Messerschmitt went to the left when he started to take off, and he was unable to control it. As a result, he performed a wheelie and broke the plane, a leg of the landing gear and the propeller, although fortunately he was unharmed. A day later, during a shot, Lieutenant Urquiola brushed the tip of the left plane against the ground and damaged it. Three days later, Lieutenant Medrano also touched the ground with one of his aircraft's planes upon landing and damaged it. Flights then had to be suspended, as not a single plane was still operational.

Finally, the Spanish unit managed to get the 15 Bf 109 F-2s. Three patrols were formed with them. The first was with Nos 1 to 5, the second with Nos 6 to 10, and the third with Nos 11 to 15. These numbers were painted in black with white trim. The emblem that had been adopted by the 2nd Squadron was painted on the cowling: a Cross of Santiago (in red), on which was the emblem (in white and blue) of Commander Joaquín García Morato's Blue Patrol, already carried by the squadron's predecessor. On 28 May, the whole squadron flew for the first time.

On the vast plain where the Spanish airfield is located, a soldier guides the pilot of a Bf 109 F-2 to his take-off position.

The black Bf 109 F-2 No.1 prepares for a new combat mission. This is the same aircraft that has the words '*CAPITÁN NORIEGA ¡Presente!*' painted on its starboard side.

On 4 June, a simulation of escorting a Ju 87 formation was carried out with complete success by the Spanish pilots. On 8 June, after some four months, the training of the 2nd Squadron was completed. Nine days later, the squadron would leave for its base of operations at the Orel-West airfield, about 360km south-west of Moscow.

At 11:15 on 17 June, the Junkers Ju 52 piloted by Lieutenant Hermenegildo Menéndez, known as '*Paco el Minero*', took off. It carried Lieutenant Barañano, Ensign Navarro, Brigadier Palacín, seven NCOs, four of whom were mechanics, two armourers, a radio operator, a soldier and a German interpreter, as well as *Oberstleutnant* von Sander, head of the *Luftwaffe* staff attached to the squadron and its liaison with the German command.

Fifteen minutes after the Ju 52, the Bf 109 F-2s began to take off in patrols. First was the 4th Patrol with three planes: Major Julio Salvador (No.13) as commander and Lieutenant Arango (No.7) and Ensign Bengoa (No.12) as wingmen. It was followed by the 1st Patrol, under the command of Captain Antonio Noriega (No.1), flying with Lieutenants Escudé (No.4), Ripollés (No.3) and Garret (No.5). Then followed the 2nd Patrol, commanded by Captain Bengoechea (No.6), flying with Lieutenants Pérez Galdós (No.10) and Robles (No.8) and Ensign Lafuente (No.9). Last was the 3rd Patrol, commanded by Captain Serra (No.11), flying with Lieutenants Medrano (No.14) and Arraiga (No.15) and Ensign Beriaín (No.2).

Captain Noriega preparing to take off in his black Bf 109 F-2 ('*Zacuto*') No.1 for a combat mission.

Due to the poor visibility, the planes adopted a whiting formation while flying over the course of the Oder River, which changed to combat formation once visibility increased and lasted until their arrival at the Stolp airfield, where they landed and spent the night. The next day, they took off for Königsberg, where they landed after a 45-minute flight and where Lieutenant Barañano and Ensign Navarro replaced Lieutenant Arango and Ensign Bengoa in their *Zacutos*, the latter moving to the Ju 52 liaison plane. They then took off for the Neukhuhren field, where they landed, refuelled and took off again for the Wilna field. There, they landed without any problems, but, during the taxiing, Lieutenant Ripollés (better known as '*El Maño*') entered an area of soft earth and overturned, resulting in a deep head wound, for which he was sent to the Wilna hospital for a few days.

On 20 June, the flight continued. They took off early in the morning for the Bobruisk airfield, now in Russia, except for Lieutenant Escudé, whose propeller brushed the ground on take-off and was unable to take off, and Ensign Navarro, whose water radiator shut down and who decided to stay behind to repair the fault. The rest of the 2nd Squadron landed safely at Bobruisk to refuel, but the persistence of bad weather forced them to remain there until the following day.

On the morning of 21 June, at just after 10:30, they took off and went into combat formation, as they were to fly over territory where the communist partisans were operating. When the formation landed in Bryansk, Lieutenant Pérez Galdós's plane (No.10) put its left wheel in a hole and crashed, resulting in a fractured left forearm and a head wound for

Two mechanics during the overhaul of a Bf 109 F-2 engine. In the foreground is a helmet with the Spanish coat of arms, a gas mask box and a Mauser 98K.

the pilot. After refuelling, they took off again and finally reached their destination, the Orel airfield. They were duly billeted and awaited Major Karl-Gottfried Nordmann, head of JG 51, to whom they were to report, which happened a few hours later. The name of the squadron within the *Luftwaffe* was '15.(Span)/JG 51'. The Spanish fighter squadron (*Spanische Jagdstaffel*) was operationally assigned to *II. Gruppe* and was deployed at the junction of the southern flank of Army Group Centre and the northern flank of Army Group South. Operationally, JG 51 and thus the Blue Squadron were dependent on *Luftwaffe* Command East (*Luftwaffenkommando Ost*).

As mentioned, the Spanish Bf 109 Fs were accompanied by a Spanish Ju 52, with the Spanish pilots in *Luftwaffe* uniform and the aircraft bearing *Luftwaffe* insignia. This was because the squadron was assigned a Junkers Ju 52/3m aircraft owned by the Spanish airline Iberia, which flew the Berlin–Blue Squadron–Blue Division route as both a liaison and courier aircraft for the two Spanish expeditionary units in Russia since one was in the northern sector and the other in the central sector. In fact, the pilot of the aircraft was Lieutenant Menéndez. With the help of this Ju 52, the transfer of the Spaniards to Orel was much more comfortable.

A nice picture showing the silhouette of a Spanish Bf 109 F-2 in the vast Soviet plain.

The Ju 52 liaison has just landed, and many men are impatiently approaching it to receive mail and parcels from Spain.

The importance of the Ju 52 liaison for both the Blue Division (in the *Wehrmacht*) and the Blue Squadron (in the *Luftwaffe*) was very great, as it allowed both Spanish units to maintain contact with each other and with Spain, as well as to evacuate the wounded to hospitals in the rear.

The 2nd Expeditionary Squadron had 19 pilot officers, two mechanic officers, one mechanic NCO, 20 specialist mechanic soldiers, two armourer officers, 10 armourer soldiers, one NCO, five radio soldiers, one medical captain, one chaplain ensign, one quartermaster officer, six staff NCOs, nine driver and mechanic soldiers, one officer and 40 aviation troop soldiers. The total was therefore one commander-in-chief, 18 pilots, seven ground service officers, eight NCOs and 85 soldiers, making a grand total of 119 men.

An *Obergefreiter* belonging to the ground echelon of the Blue Squadron standing guard next to a Bf 109 F-2. The 2nd Squadron's coat of arms painted on the port side of the engine stands out in the picture

The 2nd Squadron was distributed as follows:

Staff: Commander-in-Chief Major Salvador Díaz-Benjumea and Second-in-Command Captain Noriega
1st Patrol: Captains Bengoechea and de Frutos, Lieutenants Escudé, Arango and Medrano and Ensign González Lafuente
2nd Patrol: Captain Serra, Lieutenants Ripollés, Arraiza and Robles and Ensigns Navarro and Beriain
3rd Patrol: Lieutenants Barañano, Garret, Urquiola and Martínez Pérez-Galdós and Ensign Bengoa.

It was stipulated that a pair of aircraft should always be in a state of alert. These aircraft had to be ready for take-off at short notice so that they could intervene in any risky situation. The 'alarms' were prepared from 03:00 until 19:30.

On 26 June, the patrol was designated to take off on its first mission: a free fighter over the sector assigned to the squadron, which included the cities of Shisdra, Volchow, Mzensk and Novossil. Commander Salvador and Lieutenant Garret took off, flying Nos 13 and 5, respectively, and headed for the assigned area. When they had been in the air for about an hour and were flying over their own lines, *El Chanquete* saw some aircraft and indicated this to Salvador, who headed towards them under the protection of Garret. He spotted two planes manoeuvring with German tactics but, upon approaching, realised that they were Soviet LaGG-3s and that there were also some Il-2 and DB-3 bombers escorted by another six LaGG-3s. Salvador gained altitude and began the attack, but, in the first burst, his cannon stopped firing and one of his machine guns jammed. There were no shootdowns, and the Soviets escaped in the direction of their lines.

On 27 June, the ground echelon arrived at Orel using trucks borrowed from the Germans. The 2nd Squadron was now complete.

Major Salvador Díaz-Benjumea returned temporarily to Spain, where he remained until the beginning of August to contribute his knowledge of the war in the skies over Russia to the formation of the 3rd Blue Squadron.

Captain Noriega inside his plane, preparing for take-off. From his mechanic's clothing, we can guess that the temperature was pleasant when the photo was taken, but the harsh Russian winter was soon to arrive.

Commander Julio Salvador Díaz-Benjumea leaves the cockpit of his plane smiling despite having lost part of the cockpit during his combat mission.

When Germany began its summer offensive on 28 June, Army Group Centre (where the Blue Squadron was located) was not initially involved.

On 1 July, the 2nd Squadron got its first shootdown but also suffered its first casualty. Captain Noriega and Lieutenant Robles, with Nos 14 and 12, respectively, were on alarm duty, while Lieutenant Escudé (better known as '*Buenooo*') and Ensign Bengoa were taking off to protect a Henschel Hs 126 reconnaissance aircraft. Suddenly, three Il-2s escorted by four LaGG-3s appeared and began to bomb and strafe the road linking the village of Orel to the airfield. The Spanish mechanics began to start up the Bf 109 F-2s, and, despite the imminent danger, Noriega and Robles began to take off. However, Lieutenant Robles pulled up the landing gear too early, and, due to the slow speed of his propeller, he hit the ground and failed to take off. Noriega would be the truly unlucky one. With his low speed and altitude, he was an easy target for the Soviets and was shot down eight kilometres north-west of Mzensk. Meanwhile, the combat had continued, as Escudé and Bengoa had come when they realised the presence of the enemy aircraft, as well as Captain Frutos and Ensign Beriaín, who were on standby. In the immediate combat, Captain Frutos managed to shoot down a LaGG-3, thus avenging the death of the squadron leader, and Escudé managed to touch down another. Destroying part of the rudder and seeing smoke but not the aircraft's fall, Escudé could not confirm his victory.

Captain Noriega's body was recovered and buried in the cemetery of a Panzer division in the village of Woin, located on the road from Orel to Mzensk. After the fighting, Captains Noriega and Frutos were awarded the Iron Cross 2nd Class by General Ritter von Greim. Captain Noriega would be remembered by his comrades by painting the phrase '*CAPITÁN NORIEGA ¡Presente!*' (CAPTAIN NORIEGA Present!) on the nose of the No.1 Bf 109 F-2.

Inspector Commander Salvador gave command of the 2nd Squadron to Captain Manuel Bengoechea, who, without wasting a single second, began to lead it.

Early on 5 July, Lieutenants Garret and Urquiola took off on alarm and spotted a formation of Il-2s protected by three LaGG-3s and seven I-16 *Ratas*. Trying to keep their backs to the sun, they gained altitude until, at about 2,500 metres, they managed to position themselves behind the LaGG-3s. Garret managed to hit one of them with cannon and machine-gun fire, watching it leave a long trail of smoke and plummet. Meanwhile, faced with the imminent appearance of more Soviet aircraft, the commander of JG 51 ordered all the planes to take off, so the Spaniards went. The first one was Captain Bengoechea, accompanied by Lieutenant Ripollés, heading towards the Volchow sector and entering the front with the sun on his back. Suddenly, *El Maño* saw planes below, seven DB-3 bombers at an altitude of 150m. Bengoechea

Three comrades at the grave of Captain Antonio Noriega Labat, killed in action in July 1942.

The Bf 109 F-2 previously used by Captain Noriega was painted with the words '*CAPITÁN NORIEGA ¡Presente!*' (CAPTAIN NORIEGA Present!) on the engine (starboard side) in his memory.

positioned himself behind one of them that was breaking formation and began to shoot at it with his machine guns. As it was still a little far away, he then approached it and shot at it with his cannon, hitting its left engine, which exploded. He continued firing at it and saw its left plane catch fire. The bomber lost altitude and crashed to the north of Volchow. Ripollés then attacked another DB-3 but failed to shoot it down.

At the same time, Lieutenant Barañano and Ensign Lafuente, flying Nos 8 and 13, respectively, had spotted other DB-3s that were not only bombing but also dropping propaganda leaflets, so they took advantage of the occasion and went after them. Barañano attacked the one on the right wing of the formation, which began to smoke and from which one of its crewmen jumped, plummeting and crashing to the ground.

The other pilots were not so lucky. Escudé was hit while attacking a Pe-2 formation and was forced to parachute, falling into his own lines and being recovered by a Fieseler Fi 156 *Storch*, but what really hurt him was not being able to claim a victory over a Pe-2, which was given as probable. Ensign Lafuente was hit on one of his propeller blades, on his left plane with a broken pitot tube and on his tail wheel, although he managed to land without further incident upon his return to the field.

On 7 July, General Ritter von Greim awarded the Iron Cross 2nd Class to Captain Bengoechea and Lieutenants Barañano and Garret for their courageous fighting against the Soviets.

Encounters with Soviet aircraft were very frequent, which allowed the number of Spanish victories to increase. The Spanish missions were usually free fighters or escorts for bombing, attack or reconnaissance aircraft. During an escort flight of the Junkers Ju 88s with which they shared an airfield, on 11 July, Ensign Beriaín was forced to land on the Bryansk field. When he took off again to return to Orel, his plane, No.6, stalled and crashed, destroying it. Fortunately, Beriaín suffered only minor injuries.

On 18 July, the 2nd Squadron obtained four victories. Two patrols, made up of Captain Bengoechea (No.3) and Lieutenant Arráiza (No.11) as the first and Lieutenant Arango (No.5) and Ensign Navarro (No.4) as the second, took off at 10:30 with a mission to protect a Focke Wulf Fw 189 reconnaissance aircraft, with which they rendezvoused over their airfield and took off towards the Belew–Kosselk sector. When they were flying at an altitude of about 3,000m over Kosjolsk, 50km behind enemy lines, they were surprised by heavy anti-aircraft reaction, which had no consequences. Shortly afterwards, they observed five LaGG-3s flying lower and preparing to attack the Fw 189, so Captain Bengoechea ordered the attack and then attacked one of them without hitting it. At the same time, he saw Lieutenant Arráiza shooting at another one, part of which came off. He then saw one of them standing alone, and, positioning himself behind its tail, he shot at and hit it, seeing it then plummet and

While the aircraft is being checked and made ready to fly again, one of the mechanics takes a drink of water.

The *Luftwaffe* was pleased to be able to show that Spanish airmen were fighting alongside them. This photograph shows several German journalists at the airfield where the Spaniards were stationed.

smoke. For his part, Lieutenant Arráiza had effectively hit the LaGG-3, as Captain Bengoechea had observed, and saw it fall into a tailspin and crash to the ground. He also watched another LaGG-3 crash, which he assumed was the one shot down by his leader.

Lieutenant Arango attacked one of them, which escaped. When he turned, he saw that he was carrying a LaGG-3 on his tail but had not realised that on *its* tail was the *Zacuto* of Ensign Navarro, who shot at the LaGG-3 at 40m and saw it catch fire and go into a tailspin. The LaGG-3s then began to whip around in order to protect each other as they gained altitude but were nevertheless given a few passes until they began to run low on fuel. Lieutenant Arango then saw a plane higher up that looked like Captain Bengoechea's. He approached it but saw that it was another LaGG-3, so he positioned himself on its tail and fired at it from below, watching it explode as its pilot parachuted out.

Unlike the 1st Blue Squadron, which was very close to the front line and therefore had frequent clashes with Soviet aircraft, the 2nd Blue Squadron, as the front line shifted farther and farther away, had fewer and fewer aerial encounters with the Soviets during August (due to the German offensive against the city of Stalingrad).

A proud Spanish soldier poses next to one of the Bf 109 F-2s of the 2nd Squadron. The coat of arms used by the Spanish on their aircraft is clearly visible. In some cases, when the aircraft were painted white for the winter, this coat of arms was no longer visible.

A stupid accident on 28 July caused the death of one of the mechanics of the 2nd Squadron. At 17:40, Beriaín was taxiing from the parking area to the take-off line in his *Zacuto*, with Corporal Tomas Zaro and Private José Muñoz mounted on the planes, as usual. But suddenly, the left wheel sank into the soft earth, and the two mechanics fell to the ground with such bad luck that Corporal Zaro crashed into the propeller, dying instantly. As with Captain Noriega, Corporal Zaro would be remembered by his comrades by painting the phrase '*CABO MECÁNICO ZARO ¡Presente!*' (CORPORAL MECHANIC ZARO Present!) on the nose of the No.7 Bf 109 F-2.

After the month of July, the 2nd Squadron had eight aircraft down for sure and two probable aircraft down. On the negative side, the squadron's casualties were beginning to mount and, unfortunately, were not over yet.

Once again, misfortune would befall the 2nd Blue Squadron. It happened on 7 August after Lieutenant Robles and Ensign Navarro took off to protect a Fw 189 in the Mzensk sector, as the Fw 189 was to film them for a *Luftwaffe* newsreel, for which reason they had already agreed on the manoeuvres they were to carry out. When they were flying a dozen kilometres from Mzensk and at a speed of 300km/h, they made a pass, tail to nose, on the Fw 189. When they turned to gain altitude, as the front line was close, Lieutenant Robles heard a loud noise and saw, on the leading edge of his right wing, Ensign Navarro's aircraft pushing him up with its rear. Robles quickly pulled the lever and tried to disengage, realising that his *Zacuto*, despite the damage, was flying well. He then saw how, some 150m below, Ensign Navarro's plane, without the cockpit canopy and with its rudder destroyed, plunged down and exploded upon hitting the ground. Shortly afterwards, Captain Bengoechea flew with a Fi 156 *Storch* to the crash site, confirming that it was indeed the Bf 109 F-2 Werk N.8252 of Ensign Navarro, whose remains were buried on 8 August in the Woin cemetery.

Five days later, precisely on 13 August, Lieutenant Escudé '*Buenooo*' was rewarded for his efforts with his first shootdown, which took place during his return from a protection flight of a Ju 87 formation with Lieutenant Urquiola as his partner. Already flying over his own lines, he observed some planes that he thought were Il-2s about to attack a German column, so, without hesitating, he attacked the first one that came within range and hit it twice, setting fire to it the second time. *Buenooo* then watched it crash.

This Bf 109 F-2, ready for take-off from the Orel airfield, bears on the starboard side of the engine the phrase '*CABO MECÁNICO ZARO ¡Presente!*' (CORPORAL MECHANIC ZARO Present!) in memory of Tomás Zaro Rubio, who died on 28 July 1942 in an accident with the aircraft's propeller.

The first victories against Soviet aircraft begin to mount as evidenced by the two victory bars over the enemy painted on the tail of this Messerschmitt.

This *Luftwaffe* reconnaissance Fw 189 prepares to take off from a Soviet airfield. Its escort aircraft were two Bf 109 F-2s of the 2nd Squadron.

Several members of 2nd Squadron inspect the wreckage of a Soviet Pe-2 shot down by the unit. At the pilot's station is Lieutenant Ramón Escudé.

On 14 August, the pair of Bf 109s flown by pilots Serra and Lafuente engaged Soviet MiG-3 fighters without being shot down. The same day, the Spanish pilots who had achieved this were awarded the insignia for having completed 20 war services.

Encounters with Soviet aircraft were not frequent, but, on 17 August, the pair (‘*Rotte*’ in *Luftwaffe* terminology) formed by Captain Frutos and his wingman, Lieutenant Garret, spotted a formation of DB-3 bombers, managing to hit one of them with their aircraft fire. The bomber was most likely shot down, but the Spaniards were unable to confirm this due to the response of the Soviet escort fighters that swooped down on them. In the end, the two Spaniards managed to escape.

An unexpected visit was received on 18 August when *Oberst* Adolf Galland and *Oberstleutnant* Gunter Lützow arrived. Both were veterans of the GCE and acquaintances of some of the Spanish pilots since then.

No less important than the pilots or mechanics were other men such as those in the kitchen. Here, the cook finishes preparing the day’s food.

This tent, prepared ‘Spanish style’, demonstrates the good humour that existed in the Spanish squadron despite the adversities.

A good day was 22 August, as Captain Bengoechea managed two shootdowns. In the first morning mission, a formation of four Spanish Bf 109s ('*Schwarm*' in German terminology) composed of Captain Bengoechea, Lieutenants Barañano and Atienza and Ensign Lafuente was escorting a formation of Ju 87s when they spotted a formation of Il-2s and dived at them. Bengoechea managed to get behind one of them and caught up with it, laughing as it fell into a wood, where it exploded. For his part, Lieutenant Barañano, who had managed to hit another Il-2, in the heat of combat, overran the front line as far as Belew, where there was a strong anti-aircraft defence that shot at him and hit him squarely in the left plane, opening up a large hole and destroying the pitot tube. The Bf 109 began to lose altitude and was difficult to pilot due to problems with warping, so Lieutenant Arráiza was able to get on its tail to protect it until it finally reached the Orel field. After refuelling, Captain Bengoechea and Lieutenant Arráiza took off again for another service to protect the Ju 87s, which passed without incident. On the way back, they spotted an enemy formation, which they tied up, and Captain Bengoechea managed to shoot down a LaGG-3, his second victory of the day and his fourth overall, making him the squadron's top shootdown man.

On 28 August, the Spanish base suffered its heaviest bombing ever, carried out by at least six Il-2s (one was shot down by a German squadron aircraft that shared the airfield with the Spanish).

During September, the development of the fighting on the Eastern Front caused the German offensive to reach the Don River and continue in the direction of Stalingrad. As a result, the front line moved away from the 2nd Squadron's base, reducing the possibility of engaging the Soviets and thus of shooting down enemy aircraft in the following months. Meanwhile, at Morón Air Base, the 3rd Squadron had already begun to organise itself. In this case, unlike the transition between the 1st and 2nd Squadrons (which had been carried out inadequately, meaning that, for some months, there were no Spanish pilots in the *Luftwaffe*), it was possible to overlap the departure of the 2nd Squadron to Spain with the arrival of the 3rd Squadron. In this way, it was thought that some 3rd Squadron pilots would arrive in Russia before the departure of the 2nd Squadron and therefore share knowledge with their veteran comrades fighting in the Russian skies. A group of NCOs and soldiers from the 3rd Squadron's ground echelon left on 17 September for Werneuchen.

In October, Inspector Commander Salvador returned to Orel after supervising the training of the 3rd Squadron in Spain. The group of NCOs and soldiers from the 3rd Squadron's ground echelon also arrived in Orel. These men from the 3rd Squadron were attached to the 2nd Squadron to learn the procedures to be used on the Russian front.

On 6 October, the monotony of the skies free of Russian aircraft was finally broken as the pair formed by Lieutenant Escudé and Ensign Lafuente intercepted an Il-2 that they managed to damage, but the Soviet aircraft managed to escape (after the first burst, the weapons on Lieutenant Escudé's aircraft stopped working).

A Spanish pilot poses next to the tail of an Il-2 shot down by the squadron. These Soviet aircraft were very difficult to shoot down because of their high resistance to enemy fire.

Several members of 2nd Squadron, sitting next to one of their aircraft, recover by eating when they can between missions.

Spanish soldiers in *Luftwaffe* uniform, with Spanish insignia on their right arm, pose for the camera during a visit to a Soviet village.

After a month and a half without a single shootdown, Captain Frutos scored a victory by shooting down a Pe-2 on 9 October when, after spotting it, he chased it with his partner, Ensign Bengoa, who gave it the first pass without getting anything. Captain Frutos then managed to get behind it and, at very close range, shoot at it with the cannon and machine guns, hitting it squarely and immediately seeing its three crew members parachute out.

On 13 October, it was the turn of Lieutenant Barañano, who flew with No.11 and was partnered by Lieutenant Robles with No.7. Both took off with the order to shoot down a captive balloon and to act as free fighters. When they were flying between lines, they saw an Il-2 that Lieutenant Robles shot at unsuccessfully. In return, he received several hits – one in the armoured windscreen, another in the left plane and a third that damaged a fuel line and caused the aircraft to catch fire during landing – but he was able to get out of it safe and sound. For his part, Lieutenant Barañano attacked the Il-2 in turn and, more fortunately, shot it down.

After these clashes, the Spaniards were once again bored and could find no rivals in the sky. The planes that were on alarm were ready from 05:45 until 16:30, and even their number was increased from two to four.

On 23 October, the 1st and 2nd Patrols of the 3rd Blue Squadron left for France to train at the St-Jean-d'Angély base, about 50km south of the port of La Rochelle. Meanwhile, the 3rd Patrol was still being prepared in Spain.

The patrols that flew daily had no encounters with Soviet aircraft in the following days, having to wait until 29 October for Captain Serra and Lieutenant Medrano's mission to escort a Fw 189. Suddenly, they noticed the presence of an aircraft, and Captain Serra dived for it. Fortunately, when he was within firing distance, he saw that it was a *Luftwaffe* Messerschmitt Bf 110. When he turned to locate Lieutenant Medrano, he heard him on the radio asking for help as he was fighting enemy fighters. Captain Serra immediately headed towards the LaGG-3s harassing his wingman and began firing at one of them, of which he saw several pieces come off. While he was waiting to see it fall, the Russians began to attack him, so he consequently put his engine in and headed back to his airfield. He could only note the LaGG-3 as probable.

In the afternoon of the same day (29 October), the patrol that was in alarm at the Spanish airfield (Captain Bengoechea and Lieutenant Medrano) was ordered to take off immediately when a formation of Soviet aircraft (seven Il-2s escorted by five LaGG-3s) approached. Captain Bengoechea wrote in his mission report:

> The *Gruppe* ordered an alarm pair to take off, as enemy aircraft were approaching on a course for Orel. I went out in a pair with Lieutenant Medrano (he was going out again two hours after the first combat) and headed east, climbing to 1,500 metres. After three or four minutes we saw seven Il-2s protected by five LaGG-3s; my first intention was to attack the Il-2s, but the fighter coming higher up attacked us and we had to fight it. I shot at one in a turn and then got on its tail; I continued to fire at it from close range with machine guns and cannon, watching it start to smoke and lose altitude, until it crashed beside the Oka River, about 30 km north-west of Orel. I returned to the field, having run out of ammunition.[2]

This was Captain Bengoechea's fifth and last victory in Russia, making him the ace of the 2nd Blue Squadron. While this engagement was taking place, a second pair of Spanish Bf 109s took off to join the fight – Captain Serra and Lieutenant Pérez-Galdós – although Lieutenant Pérez-Galdós had to land again due to mechanical problems and Captain Serra had to continue his flight alone. The LaGG-3s spotted him, and one of them launched itself at the Spaniard in an attempt to shoot him down. Fortunately for Captain Serra, he was able to use his aerial manoeuvres to get into an advantageous position against the LaGG-3 and managed to shoot down the Soviet aircraft.

The day of 29 October had been very tough after many days of no fighting with the Soviets, but no Spanish pilots were shot down, and at least two Russian planes had been shot down.

During the month of November, Germany began to suffer serious setbacks in different areas (i.e., Stalingrad, El Alamein and North Africa) that forced the displacement of part of the fighters that were deployed in the USSR. Thus, from JG 51, four squadrons were sent urgently to Tunisia at the beginning of November: *II. Gruppe* and the 3rd Squadron of *I. Gruppe*. Therefore, in the central zone of the Eastern Front, only two *Gruppen* remained: I/51 in the Vyazma area, with one squadron less and equipped with Fw 190s, and IV/51 in the Vitebsk area, still equipped with Bf 109s.

November 1942 was the last month of the 2nd Squadron's stay in Russia. On 4 November, Captain Bengoechea was decorated with the Iron Cross 1st Class. On 11 November, the last victory of the 2nd Squadron was achieved by Lieutenant Medrano, who shot down a Pe-2 while it was flying at an altitude of 7,000m and saw it fall and crash to the ground without any of its crew managing to parachute out. The same day, the Ju 52 took off for Spain, carrying Troop Lieutenant Salvador Tomé, the first officer of the 2nd Squadron to return to Spain. In the following days and until their return to Spain, the squadron carried out some services in which they only faced old I-153s but without any effective result.

2 Arráez Cerdá, 'Les Espagnols de la Luftwaffe', 18, p.46.

A well-equipped Spanish soldier belonging to the 2nd Squadron with all combat equipment. Note his emblem with the Spanish flag on his right arm and the snowy plain that made the Spanish unit's day-to-day life more difficult.

A downed Pe-2 is closely watched by men of the 2nd Squadron in search of some 'souvenirs'.

On 18 November, the first elements of the 3rd Blue Squadron arrived in Orel after their training phase in France. On 30 November, the inspector commander of the 2nd Blue Squadron handed over command to Ferrándiz, inspector commander of the 3rd Blue Squadron, concluding the intervention of the 2nd Squadron on the Russian front.

On 2 December, the first expedition of the 2nd Squadron, under the command of Captain Ripollés, left Orel for Spain. On 7 December, the second expedition of the 2nd Squadron, under the command of Lieutenant Arango, left for Spain as well.

The 2nd Blue Squadron took part in 1,312 flight missions, flying 117 air combats in which they managed to shoot down 13 enemy aircraft. On the negative side, they had three casualties: two officers (Captain Noriega and Ensign Navarro) and one corporal (Zaro).

Close-up of the badge of the 2nd Blue Squadron, comprising the emblem of Joaquín García Morato's fighter group on a red St James' Cross, on the nose of a Bf 109 F-4 belonging to 15.(Span)/JG 51.

3

3rd Squadron

In August 1942, the personnel assigned to form part of the 3rd Expeditionary Squadron in Russia were ordered to concentrate at the Morón de la Frontera airfield to carry out the planned training prior to their departure for Germany. On 1 September 1942, the 3rd Squadron was formed under the command of Major Carlos Ferrándiz Arjonilla, the only one of the Blue Squadron commanders who had no previous experience in air combat during the GCE. Their training began on 17 September in Tablada, and it was decided that the veteran pilots of the 1st Squadron would participate in the training with those of the 3rd Squadron while they were in Spain (Captain Ibarreche and Lieutenants Lacour and García introduced them to flying based on the types of training used by the *Luftwaffe*). In addition, all training was supervised by the inspector commander of the 2nd Squadron, Julio Salvador. To facilitate the arrival of the 3rd Squadron, it was decided that 3rd Squadron personnel would join the 2nd Squadron at Orel after only one month of training at Werneuchen. Thanks to this organisation, the men of the 3rd Squadron would not suffer the various problems of adapting to the Russian front that the 1st Squadron had suffered.

There, they first flew the Fiat CR.32 and then the Messerschmitt Bf 109 B-2 and E-3. The training went perfectly. However, during a landing on 17 September, the Messerschmitt Bf 109 E-3 registered '6-112' had the right wheel of its landing gear seize, causing the aircraft to do a wheelie and to flap, damaging its left wing and propeller. Likewise, on 9 October, the Bf 109 E-3 registered '6-87' took off, in this case piloted by Captain Gonzalo Hevia.

Once the squadron was concentrated in Madrid, on 21 October, the first echelon left by rail for the French border, made up of Commander Ferrándiz, Captains Asensi, Alós, Gavilán and Hevia, Lieutenants Calleja, Luca de Tena, Azqueta, Lacruz, Pérez Muñoz and Roselló and Ensigns Vara de Rey and Teixidor. On 22 October, they crossed the border, and, on 23 October, they joined the St-Jean-d'Angély airfield. For this 3rd Squadron, the Werneuchen airfield was not the one chosen to finish their training (except for the advance squadron that was sent to Orel to collaborate with the 2nd Squadron). Rather, the 1st and 2nd Patrols were deployed to the advanced fighter training base of St-Jean-d'Angély, where they would stay for approximately one month. La Rochelle was home to the training squadrons (*Ausbildung Staffeln*) of the JGs included in Supplementary Fighter Group, East (*Ergänzungs-Jagdgruppe Ost*), which provided advanced training for pilots arriving from the Fighter Schools. Under Ensign von Goestern, Brigadier Wieckert and Sergeant Scephen, instruction not only included flying the Messerschmitt Bf 109 E and F but also extended to other types of aircraft such as the Heinkel He 45 (an old acquaintance of the Spanish), the Klemm Kl 35, the Arado Ar 96 and the Focke Wulf Fw 56.

On 4 November, the ground echelon left for St-Jean-d'Angély, where it arrived the following day.

The 3rd Expeditionary Squadron had 19 pilot officers, five support corps officers, 14 NCOs and 88 soldiers. The 3rd Squadron was distributed as follows:

Staff: Commander-in-Chief Major Carlos Ferrándiz Arjonilla
1st Patrol: Captains Asensi and Gavilán, Lieutenants Calleja, García, Pérez and Roselló and Ensign Teixidor
2nd Patrol: Captains Alós and Hevia and Lieutenants Luca de Tena, Azqueta Lacruz and Martínez
3rd Patrol: Captains Gracía and Ozores, Lieutenants Pérez and Meneses and Ensigns Guibert and Aldecoa
Pilots of the 2nd Squadron who remained temporarily in service with the 3rd Squadron: Lieutenants Beriain, Barañano, Bengoa, Garret, Martínez and Urquiola.

Of the squadron's pilots, only Lieutenant Luca de Tena had achieved an aerial victory in the GCE, although some other pilots had flown fighters, attack aircraft or seaplanes during the Spanish conflict. This was the case with Captain Hevia, who, coming from the seaplanes, became a great fighter pilot.

The Oath of Allegiance to the *Führer* for the campaign against communism took place on 11 November, presided over by *Hauptmann* Lonnel, head of the school, and attended by Lieutenant Colonel José Pazó Montes, air attaché in Berlin.

Several members of the 3rd Squadron's ground echelon form up in their German uniforms. The efforts of these men proved vital to the squadron's survival in combat.

Captain Hevia lights a cigarette upon his return from combat. With 12 victories, this pilot was the greatest ace of all the Spanish pilots of the five Blue Squadron.

After completing their training on 13 November, the pilots left for Berlin the next day, where they completed their equipment at the *Luftwaffe* Quartermaster's Office. On 17 November, they flew to the Tempelhoff airfield and then, in the Ju 52 liaison, piloted by *Paco el Minero*, flew to the front. They stopped at Warsaw for refuelling and continued to Baranowichtz, where they spent the night. The next day, they flew to Minsk, and, after refuelling there, they finally took off for the Orel airfield, where their comrades of the 2nd Squadron awaited relief. For their part, the ground echelon made a slow journey that ended on 29 November with their arrival at Orel.

Finally, on 1 December, the official relief took place, which was partial and staggered so as to not paralyse the action at the front. For this purpose, pilots from the 2nd Squadron were added to the 3rd Squadron for three months: Lieutenants Barañano, Garret, Urquiola and Pérez Galdós and Ensigns Bengoa and Beriaín, as well as a small group of specialists. They also 'inherited' 14 Messerschmitt Bf 109 F-2 aircraft from the previous squadron, 10 of which were flying and four under repair.

The 3rd Squadron was organised into a main squadron and three patrols of six pilots each, and, like the 2nd Squadron, in the *Luftwaffe*, it was given the designation '15.(Span)/JG 51'. For its part, the *Luftwaffe* added a few men under the command of *Hauptmann* Holz: *Leutnant* Prang as quartermaster, *Oberfeldwebel* Fresse as accountant, *Stabsfeldwebel* Zimmermann and Brann as depot keepers, *Stabsfeldwebel* Hombach, Jann, Fiel, Fuster, Frowein, Gachr and Teschendorff as interpreters and *Oberfeldwebel* Zacharias as clerk, as well as *Unteroffiziere* Gairnnert, Wienker and Schinitt and Health *Unteroffizier* Grambar and Remll.

When all the 3rd Squadron pilots finally arrived at the front, the 2nd Squadron pilots were repatriated. It was on 1 December that the pilots of the 3rd Patrol began to join the rest of the men of the 3rd Squadron, although the unit was not complete until March 1943, when the pilots of the 2nd Squadron who were attached to the 3rd Squadron returned to Spain.

The first flights were orientation and reconnaissance ones and consisted of two pilots (one from the 2nd Squadron and one from the 3rd Squadron).

The morning of 1 December 1942 dawned very cold but with good visibility, and, at about 09:00, a Russian reconnaissance plane appeared over the vertical field, which was shot at by the German flak battery, putting it to flight. Before that, at 08:15, the squadron commanders, Captains Bengoechea (No.2 *Zacuto*) and Andrés Asensi Álvarez-Arenas (No.15

The 3rd Blue Squadron's ground echelon arriving at Orel on 29 November 1942.

The Russian winter has arrived, as shown by the coat of white paint on the aircraft and the warm clothing of the Spanish pilots of the 3rd Squadron posing for the photographer next to an aircraft still wearing the insignia of the 2nd Squadron. From left to right: Lieutenant Azqueta, Ensign Teixidor, Captain Alós and Lieutenants Pérez Muñoz, Calleja and Lacruz.

Zacuto), had taken off both to protect a Fw 189 that was to carry out reconnaissance over the Mzensk sector and for Captain Asensi to begin familiarising himself with the area of operations. Thus, while they were waiting for the Fw 189, they received a communication from the airfield informing them that the Fw 189 would not attend the rendezvous so that they could perform the service as free fighters. They were also informed of the presence of enemy aircraft over the city of Orel and found that it was a Yak-9. When Captain Bengoechea was about to attack, he heard his partner on the radio saying that he had lost his way and that his engine had broken down.

At the airfield, the radio service that had heard this communication began to radio a course to Captain Asensi, who did not listen and limited himself to saying that he barely had any visibility because his windscreen was covered with oil, and so on until nothing was heard. Shortly afterwards, a communication was received from the *Wehrmacht* informing them that a Bf 109 had fallen three kilometres inside enemy lines. The 3rd Squadron had just lost its commander-in-chief, who would not return to Spain until 2 April1954, when he was repatriated together with members of the Blue Division and the *Waffen-SS*, also prisoners, on the ship *SEMIRAMIS*, chartered by the International Red Cross. Consequently, the command of the 3rd Squadron fell to Captain Antonio Alós Herrero, as he was the oldest captain.

The Spanish squadron's area of action covered from Kirov (30 geographic degrees from the base) to Liwny (120 geographic degrees), the nearest front area being Mzensk. As had happened to the 2nd Squadron, during the month of December, the main combats of the Russian front were centred in the Stalingrad area, so air clashes with the Soviets were scarce.

On 2 December, with no services due to bad weather, the first expedition of the 2nd Squadron, under the command of recently promoted Captain José Mª Ripollés '*El Maño*', set off for Spain.

The components of the ground echelon were beginning to have serious problems due to the low temperatures, which sometimes reached minus 40 degrees Celsius. The cold made it very difficult to start the aircraft engines, which was solved, at least to a large extent, thanks to generators that injected hot air. Given the Spanish idiosyncrasy, these generators were immediately nicknamed '*Las Cachondas*' (The Horny Ones).

Above: Captain Antonio Alós (white jacket) and his mechanic in conversation at the snowy Orel airfield at the end of December 1942. Behind them is a Bf 109 F of the 3rd Squadron in winter camouflage.
Right: E. Demetrio Bravo, 3rd Squadron radio mechanic, in typical *Luftwaffe* uniform. He later also served time with the 4th Squadron.

In the following days, services could not be carried out or were aborted due to the prevailing bad weather.

On 7 December, it was the turn of the second echelon of the 2nd Squadron, under the command of Lieutenant José Arango López, to return to Spain.

The morning of 8 December dawned with an alarm that enemy aircraft were heading towards the airfield. The service pair took off immediately, and their mere presence in the air caused the Russian aircraft to turn back, disappearing into their own territory. Later, Fw 189s were protected without incident. The highlight of the day, however, was the news that Captain Asensi was taken prisoner and still alive, which was learnt from a Russian prisoner.

On 9 December, an Il-2 strafed the side of the Spanish airfield but did not cause any damage. 10 December was a public holiday, as it was the feast of the Virgin of Loreto (patron saint of Spanish aviators). In the morning, the Spaniards took off to protect a Fw 189 in the Bachow sector, which ended happily. This was followed by a party in the airfield theatre, with entertainment and an orchestra. The Spaniards brought their stocks of wine and cognac, and the Germans a few bottles of French champagne, which were received with the honours they deserved. The temperature there reached many degrees, while outside it was minus 30 degrees Celsius.

On 15 December, as the fog thinned, Captain Gonzalo Hevia Álvarez de Quiñones and Lieutenant Carmelo Lacruz left for the Smolensk field to take over two new Bf 109 F-2s for the squadron. The next day, Captain Hevia arrived with his Bf 109 F-2, but Lieutenant Lacruz did not make it since a wheel of his landing gear got stuck in the soft ground, preventing him from taking off.

There was some activity on 17 December with an alarm take-off, although the enemy aircraft could not be located. This was followed by a protection service of a Henschel Hs 126 in the Uljanowo sector, which always proved tricky due to the different characteristics and performances of the two types of aircraft and culminated the day with the presence of Russian aircraft dropping propaganda leaflets over the field. In the following days, bad weather conditions prevented flights from taking place.

Christmas was celebrated on 24 December. Finally, on 27 December, the squadron's first two victories were achieved. The first took place when the alarm pair of Lieutenant Barañano, 2nd Squadron, and Lieutenant Lacruz, 3rd Squadron, took off to attack an Il-2 attacking *Werhmacht* troops. They soon spotted two Il-2s and headed towards them. Once positioned behind them, at the signal from Barañano, Lacruz fired, at about 100m, his machine guns and cannon at the one on the left. After he got off its tail to avoid crashing into it, his windscreen was covered in oil, and he watched as some smoking pieces of the Il-2 came off. He then lost sight of it and took the opportunity to clean his windscreen and check that everything was in perfect order. Then, with Barañano behind him, they saw the Il-2s escaping again. Lacruz managed to get behind them and fired again with everything he had until he pulled back. However, when he turned left, he received several hits that left him without a radio, compass and anemometer and with the water radiator thermostat on full blast. Without hesitation, and using his pocket compass, Lacruz set a course for his airfield, gradually losing altitude with great difficulty but fortunately managing to land next to a German flak battery, only one kilometre from the Soviet lines. Later, upon his return, he was enthusiastically welcomed by his comrades, as he had achieved the squadron's first victory. For his part, Barañano was unlucky since, although he managed to hit his Il-2 several times, he did not manage to shoot it down.

At the same time, in another sector of the front, Lieutenant Ramón Luca de Tena y Laso and Ensign Fernando Bengoa Clemares (2nd Squadron) were on free fighter duty, flying at about 2,000m over Nowosil, when they spotted an aircraft flying at a higher altitude than them and leaving a long trail of water vapour behind it. Ensign Bengoa put his engine into full throttle, quickly gained altitude and managed to catch up with it, learning that it was a Pe-2 over the town of Mzensk. Upon seeing him, it turned north-west in an attempt to reach his lines. Already over enemy territory, Bengoa climbed 300m above the Soviet and, with the sun at his back, began a dive while firing cannon and machine-gun fire. He did not stop doing so until he was about 20m from it, clearly seeing how his shots were embedded in its planes and engines and how it then plunged to the ground, exploding some 20km north-west of Minsk.

The bad weather then continued to persist, and the year 1942 ended without any further developments. Thanks to the two shootdowns on 27 December, the 3rd Squadron ended the year with two victories.

The year 1943 also began with hellish weather that prevented any aerial activity, so it was decided to hold a football match between the Spanish and the Germans with whom they shared the airfield. Due to the state of the terrain, ice and snow, the match ultimately turned into a 'pitched battle' that ended with everyone happy, content and wanting to play again as soon as the occasion arose, which would only happen a few more times.

However, while the members of the 3rd Squadron were having fun, several hundred kilometres away, a Spanish aircraft was attacked. The Orel area was heavily populated by Soviet guerrillas, who made the tasks of the German rearguard units difficult and affected the air units. Specifically, on New Year's Day 1943, the Spanish Ju 52 piloted by Lieutenant Hermenegildo Menéndez, which was carrying mail and parcels, was wounded in its left heel by shots fired by the guerrillas while the plane was flying at low altitude towards the Siverskaya airfield, near Leningrad, where the

Lieutenant Hermenegildo Menéndez '*Paco el Minero*' (pilot of the Ju 52 that linked the Blue Division and the Blue Squadron with the rearguard) and Aviation Troop Lieutenant Fernando Tomé with nurses from the Blue Division.

Blue Division was located. The pilot's skill allowed him to land at Ostrovo without major damage, where he was quickly treated and given an injection to prevent infection, after which he was ordered to continue towards his destination. He was then hospitalised in Berlin, where he remained until 12 March, when he was discharged and returned to Spain.

As with previous squadrons, a pair of aircraft was kept on standby to react quickly to any approaching enemy.

In the following days, the bad weather continued to persist, although some services were carried out. On 6 January, they went out to protect an Fw 189 in the Arckanjelskoje sector but had to return without being able to finish it. On 11 January, there were several sorties due to an alarm, but they were unsuccessful, although, during one of them, Ensign Alfonso Teixidor failed to take off due to the state of the terrain but was unharmed and the aircraft slightly damaged.

On 12 January, there was an alarm take-off. Lieutenant Pérez Galdós did it without any problems, but his colleague Lieutenant Carmelo Lacruz Cuervo took off almost in a stall, and, when he was about 20m above the ground, the Bf 109 F-2 inverted on the runway and was destroyed. When rescue immediately arrived, Lieutenant Lacruz was found almost unconscious and with a jet of petrol pouring over his face, which was causing severe intoxication. As it was impossible to get him out of the plane since his legs were trapped, an iron was placed to deflect the jet of petrol. When a team of specialists managed to free him, it was found that he had several fractures, the most serious being a broken right femur. Consequently, he was taken to the hospital in Orel, where he received his first treatment and was then evacuated by plane to the hospital in Könisberg.

The squadron had lost two pilots in a short time and had only achieved two aerial victories, so the morale of the squadron was not very high. It was necessary for victories to begin to be achieved for the squadron's dynamic to improve, and it did not take long for this to happen.

The following days continued as before. On 15 January, the thermometer reached minus 40 degrees Celsius, but, at 10:00, the Spaniards sortied to protect a Fw 189 over Mzensk. On 16 January, an alarm and free fighter sortie was conducted without sighting enemy aircraft. The next day, an Fw 189 was escorted again, this time in the Arckanjelskoje sector, and they also went out on free fighter duty, without any results. The weather continued to impede war services until 23 January, when the weather improved a little and they left to protect a formation of He 111s over Liwny, which five LaGG-3s tried to attack. The Soviets were intercepted by Lieutenant Calleja, who engaged them in combat, but the LaGG-3s escaped without damage.

The next day dawned with better weather, and soon the alarm pair went out but did not find the enemy, and Captain Gonzalo Hevia had to return due to engine failure. Later, there were other services to protect their own aircraft in the Arckanjelskoje sector and free fighter, which went on as normal, although they did not manage to spot any enemy aircraft.

The following days passed more or less in the same way, but 27 January turned out to be a memorable day for the squadron. In the first service of the day, Lieutenant Emilio Barañano Martínez (2nd Squadron) and Ensign Miguel Martínez Vara de Rey (3rd Squadron) took off on free fighter duty, and, shortly afterwards, they spotted a formation of Pe-2 aircraft. When they managed to get behind them, the Spaniards fired on the last of the formation. Vara de Rey hit one of the Pe-2s, which spun down in flames and crashed to the ground, although two of its three crewmen managed to parachute out. Meanwhile, the Pe-2 that Barañano had attacked had its right engine catch fire when it was hit by the first shots and fell into a steep dive, crashing to the ground. Then, squeezed between the Soviet formation, they began to attack the others. Barañano attacked one of them with all his guns from a few metres away, and it began to emit black smoke and started a dive, separating from the formation, but its fate was sealed. The veteran Spanish pilot, with 67 war services in the 2nd Squadron, began a turn, chasing it and giving it two passes, the last of which made it fall to the ground, where he strafed it again for total destruction. Barañano watched how two of its crew members abandoned it and fled quickly. Vara de Rey also attacked another Pe-2 and managed to shoot it down despite having exhausted the ammunition in his cannon.

The day's good fortune had not ended, for also in the air was the pair formed by Captain Gonzalo Hevia Álvarez de Quiñones, who would become the top ace of all the Spanish pilots in Russia, and Ensign Beriain, another 2nd Squadron veteran with 85 war services. According to Captain Hevia:

> We were flying a typical protection mission of an Fw 189, a reconnaissance aircraft, with an asymmetrical glazed cockpit and double fuselage with two rudders. It flew at low speed, reconnoitring the front, and we were to protect it and warn it of danger if Russians came to attack it. Upon reaching the Jelez sector, my point man, Ensign Beriain, spotted some trails that he alerted me to. As I tried to observe them and was distracted for a moment, I saw a formation of three aircraft heading to attack the Fw 189: they were LaGG-3 fighters. I ordered my point to attack the lowest one, while I did the same with the highest one, which at that moment was turning to get on the tail of our reconnaissance aircraft. I banked my Messerschmitt to the right, collimated him very correctly and fired. That pilot did not know what he was doing, he got in front of me and I watched as he went into the jet of fire from the hub to the tail, starting to smoke. It crashed to the ground; you could say it shot itself down.[1]

1 Arráez Cerdá, 'Les Espagnols de la Luftwaffe', 18, p.60.

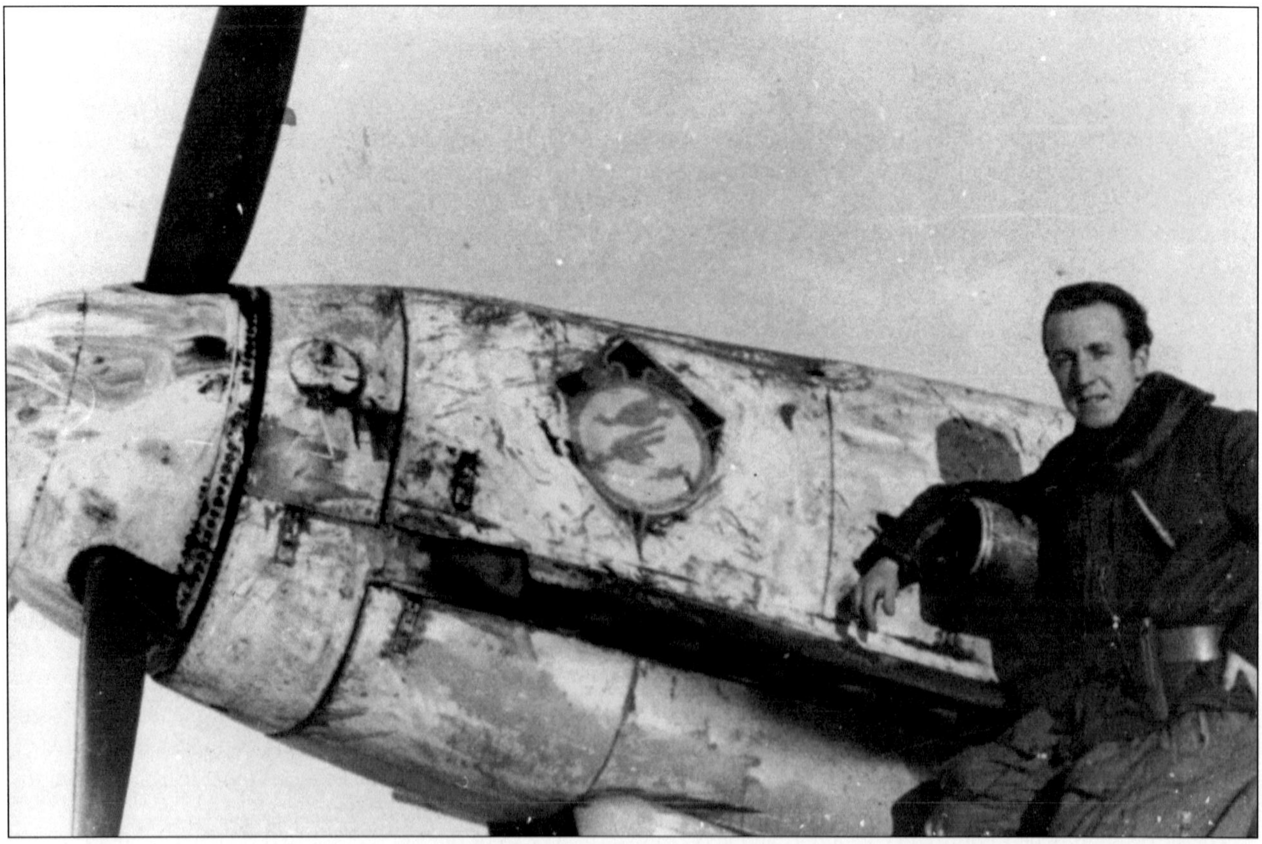

Upon arriving at the Orel airfield, Lieutenant Miguel Martínez Vara de Rey poses for the photographer next to a Bf 109 F-2 'inherited' from the 2nd Squadron (as can be seen by the emblem painted on the engine).

For his part, Ensign Beriain positioned himself at the tail of his LaGG-3, which, locked onto what it thought was a sure victim, the Fw 189, did not detect the presence of the *Zacuto*. Beriain opened fire and saw his shots hit the cockpit and the planes of the Soviet aircraft, which began to dive and crashed to the ground.

As the two pilots congratulated each other on their shootdowns, they saw six other LaGG-3s also trying to attack the Fw 189. Beriain realised that the last LaGG-3 in the formation had spotted him, and he moved in until he was on its tail and a little lower and managed to hit it with his first shots, which sent it into a tailspin with a thick trail of smoke.

After the landing, there was great joy in the field, for seven kills in one day was a formidable thing. The 3rd Squadron's morale was boosted after flying almost two months of combat missions with little success.

On 28 January, services began early in the morning with a protection mission against Heinkel He 111 bombers, during which Captain Alos and Lieutenant Calleja fought against five LaGG-3s, exhausting their ammunition without being able to shoot them down and being forced to return to the airfield. Meanwhile, when Lieutenant Roselló was starting his take-off upon returning from a service, his engine cut out, and his aircraft collapsed and capsized. Fortunately, the injuries he received were not serious, and, after his first treatment at the Orel hospital, he was evacuated to another hospital in Poland, where he recovered quickly. In addition, the camp was bombed twice that day, one of which hit one of the fuel tanks, but the attacks did not cause any casualties among the Spaniards.

On 30 January, Captain Gavilán Ponce de León and wingman Lieutenant Pérez Muñoz were flying on free fighter duty when, some 20km south of Jelez, they spotted two aircraft flying very low and that were barely distinguishable in their white camouflage. Before attacking, Gavilán decided to give them a pass to check if they were indeed enemy, which they both did, and found that they were Polikarpov I-153s, on which they could make out the red star. They repeated the pass, and Gavilán fired on the one on the left, which fell to the ground, where both pilots gave it another pass to ensure its destruction. Then, with their tanks almost empty, they returned to the airfield.

On 31 January, the Ju 52 arrived with letters and parcels from Spain, which made everyone very happy, especially because of the Christmas bonus that the company *Construcciones Aeronáuticas SA* (CASA) had sent to the squadron members, which they received two months late.

February confirmed what had been suspected since January, namely that Russian aircraft were once again appearing in the Orel area. Evidently, the German failure at Stalingrad was the spark that started the definitive change in the war effort on the Eastern Front. This situation meant that the number of combat missions flown by Spanish pilots also increased, although the bad weather meant that few combat missions were flown in the first half of February.

Black *Zacutos* Nos 16 and 12 prepare to take off from the snowy Orel airfield in January 1943. In the background are several Fw 190s belonging to a German unit also based at Orel.

Three of the best pilots of the 3rd Blue Squadron at the Orel airfield: Pérez Muñoz, Teixidor and Aldecoa.

On 2 February, a formation of He 111s was protected over the sector between the Jewhamwkossorsk road to the Solotuchino and Kossorska railway stations. On this mission, Lieutenant Calleja's engine stalled during the approach to the airfield, resulting in damage to the aircraft, although the pilot was unhurt.

On 5 February, which dawned with better weather after a bombing that caused no casualties among the Spaniards, indirect protection services were provided to a group of *Stukas* in the Maloarckangelsk sector, during which Commander Ferrandiz and Captain Alos attacked seven Il-2s. However, their escort fighter appeared, combat ensued, and the Spaniards soon had to turn back, both because they were short of fuel and because they had run out of ammunition. The following day, the escort of the *Stukas* was repeated, this time in the Kurut sector. On 9 February, the Ju 88s went out on free fighter and protection missions, without encountering any enemy.

Soviet troops were getting closer and closer to Orel, and Soviet bombing raids on the Spanish air base become frequent. The Soviets came to occupy Rjev and Vyazma but were finally stopped by German troops. Despite this, the missions entrusted to the Spaniards continued to be carried out daily. On 15 February, the weather did not improve; despite this, several protection flights were made for the *Stukas* in the Kurut and Maloarckangelsk sectors.

But the Russian ground offensive continued, and the squadron was ordered to have the most essential equipment ready in case the order to evacuate the airfield was given at any given moment. At the same time, German bomb squadrons placed three 500kg bombs in each of the arcades of the base's buildings, set to explode in case of evacuation. Fortunately, however, this did not happen, as the Germans reinforced the Orel sector with 18 divisions. In the ensuing fighting, the Soviets managed to occupy Rzhev and Viazma but did not manage to advance any farther, and the front remained stable until the summer of 1943.

On 17 February, five of the seven pilots who made up the last echelon joined the squadron: Captain Ruy Ozores Ochoa '*El Barón*', Lieutenants Bernardo Meneses Orozco and Alejandro Pérez González and Ensigns Vicente Aldecoa Lecanda and Javier Mª Guibert Amor, as well as Quartermaster Lieutenant Rafael Soler Rodero. Captain Hevia, who had gone to

Lieutenant Alejandro Pérez González posing with his Bf 109 F-2. During his service with the 3rd Squadron, he managed to shoot down an enemy aircraft.

Lieutenant Javier Mª Guibert of the 3rd Squadron posing with his *Zacuto*. This pilot achieved two victories, one with the 3rd Squadron and the second while attached to the 4th Squadron.

Berlin to pick them up, also arrived with them. Consequently, the following day, under the command of Lieutenant Barañano and Ensign Bengoa, the specialist personnel of the 2nd Squadron who had remained attached to the 3rd Squadron returned to Spain by rail. However, since the weather had improved that day, protection services were carried out in the Trozan, Alesejwka and Kurut sectors. Only one incident occurred when Ensign Guibert had problems upon take-off but without consequences.

On 19 February, Captain Antonio Alós Herrero and Ensign Miguel Martínez Vara de Rey strafed enemy troop concentrations in the Pokrowskoje sector, where the Russians were attacking most intensely.

The following day, the weather deteriorated, although two services to protect the Ju 87s in the Kamenka sector were successfully carried out. Interestingly, on this day, each member of the squadron received a bottle of French champagne and another of Marie Brizard aniseed.

The increase in ground fighting was soon noticeable in the air. Thus, shortly before dawn on 22 February, the order was given to begin services of all kinds. Major Carlos Ferrándiz Arjonilla, flying with Ensign Vara de Rey as point, attacked a formation of nine Il-2s escorted by four LaGG-5s, which the Spaniards saw for the first time on this front, but to no avail. Captain Alós also engaged in combat with LaGG-5s during an escort of the *Stukas* in the Bolchow sector, and Lieutenant Rafael Calleja González-Camino fought with LaGG-5s while protecting a formation of He 111s, in both cases without any results.

While all this was going on, Captain Hevia and Ensign Aldecoa observed some aircraft that Captain Hevia mistook for Fw 190s. As they approached closer, he realised his mistake – they were the new and more modern LaGG-5s. Hevia positioned himself behind and below the tail of one, and, at about 50m away, he fired a burst that hit it squarely and made it fall, crashing to the ground. The fight had not lasted even half a minute.

In the vicinity, the pair formed by Major Ferrándiz and Lieutenant Julio Manuel Pérez Muñoz were flying on free fighter duty when they spotted a formation of Il-2s over enemy territory and began to pursue them. The lieutenant managed to position himself behind the last one on the right and shot at it with his cannon, hitting it and seeing it separate from the group. He then repeated the attack, and the Il-2 began a dive, plunging to the ground. For his part, the commander attacked another of the Il-2s, but despite having hit him, he did not fall and instead fled, flying with difficulty at ground level to avoid another attack.

It was not yet dawn on 23 February when the alarm patrol took off for Ju 87 protection over Shisdra and Bolchow, as enemy air activity was progressively increasing. Meanwhile, the order to take off was received in view of the appearance of Il-2 aircraft attacking *Wehrmacht* troops, so Captain Hevia and Ensign Aldecoa, who made up the second alarm patrol, left. When they flew over Borowitch, Captain Hevia saw a formation of five Il-2s being protected by five LaGG-5s. He recalled that:

> I had a feeling that, once we got to the front, we would find enemy fighters, and we did. We saw a formation of about five Il-2s attacking the ground troops by whiting and protected by about five LaGG-5s. In this situation we could not attack the Il-2s, so I told Aldecoa to stick with me and we started to take altitude to be able to fight with the LaGGs. The LaGGs made a very strange manoeuvre, one of them dropped off and attacked me from the side and with very little correction, disappearing towards their lines. I took advantage of the Russians' confusion and told the Ensign that we should attack the Il-2s. We levered up and dived towards them. One of them must have seen us and broke away, so I approached him and began to shoot at him from about 150 metres in a left turn, until he straightened out and continued in a straight flight. I then positioned myself behind him, firing, until I overtook him by overshooting. I tightened the turn to the left and saw the enemy aircraft lose altitude, until it landed and caught fire after a short while. I looked for Aldecoa and was horrified to see that he was attacking another Il-2 but instead of passing it, firing and picking up again, he slowed down and stayed in formation with them. I understood this manoeuvre, as it was one of his first engagements.[2]

In the Shisdra sector, Lieutenant Rafael Calleja and Ensign Vara de Rey were flying and spotted three Il-2s just as an Fw 190 was shooting down one of them. The other two took off in different directions, and Vara de Rey began to fire on the closest one and damaged it. He then turned and positioned himself behind Calleja, who in turn fired on the Russian until he ran out of ammunition. Vara de Rey relieved him and gave it another three passes, hitting it completely on the last one. The Il-2 then lost pieces of its wing and fell to the ground, where it exploded.

Shortly afterwards, while Captain Gavilán and Lieutenant Pérez Muñoz were returning to their field, they received an alarm about seven Il-2s. The captain radioed his wingman, and the latter replied that he had just seen the red light for being low on fuel. Gavilán ordered him to continue towards the airfield and, without wasting a second, headed for the alarm area himself. He immediately spotted the Il-2s that were attacking and moved into their formation, quickly firing at the nearest one, destroying a wing and making it crash. During this action, he was attacked by a LaGG-3, from which

2 Arráez Cerdá, 'Les Espagnols de la Luftwaffe', 18, p.62.

he escaped with a quick turn, heading without delay towards Orel since his own red low fuel light had already been on for a few minutes.

The day had ended with three more aircraft shot down, bringing the 3rd Squadron's victory tally to 15 in return for one pilot lost and one seriously wounded.

The personnel of the squadron's last echelon, with specialists and ground personnel, arrived by rail in Orel on 24 February under the command of Captain José Antonio García-Alfonso Menéndez-Conde and Lieutenant Narciso García García. With them arrived a good quantity of supplies from the Spanish Quartermaster's Office, which made everyone very happy. They were already very tired of the German Quartermaster's Office and were eager to enjoy a good Spanish meal, which they were able to do for a while thanks to the supplies they received.

On this day, despite the overcast skies, there was not a moment's rest, and the services continued uninterrupted. Ju 87s and He 111s were protected in the Shisdra area, and, between the two services, the entire front was patrolled in free fighters.

During one of the protection services of the *Stukas*, Major Ferrándiz and Lieutenant Azqueta spotted a group of 12 Pe-2s, so they attacked them. The commander positioned himself over one of them, which was flying at an altitude of about 300m, and shot it down. He climbed again and positioned himself over another Pe-2, which he damaged with several bursts and started to release black smoke from its left engine. However, when he was about to finish it off, his cannon jammed, and, with no ammunition for his machine guns and since he was well within enemy lines, he decided to break off the fight and could not pinpoint the place where the Pe-2 crashed. Lieutenant Azqueta, in turn, fired on another of the Pe-2s once he was behind its tail, checking through the tracers how his shots were embedded in the fuselage and planes. He then used his cannon, and his impacts produced explosions in the Pe-2, which began to make strange movements. He fired at it again, setting fire to its left engine and causing it to crash in a forest to the north of Shisdra.

During another protection of the Ju 87s, Captain Hevia, who had Ensign Aldecoa as wingman, saw a formation of LaGG-3s and headed towards it. He positioned himself behind the one that seemed the most isolated and fired at it until the Russian began to reverse with the intention of escaping and started a dive that it could not get out of, crashing to the ground. Hevia then climbed back up and watched as the LaGG-3s attacked in formation, so he entered it, firing at one and shooting it down over a wood. Hevia had just scored his first double.

In another service, Aldecoa, flying over Shisdra, saw several Pe-2s with an escort of several LaGGs. After climbing, he attacked one of them, hitting it and sending it into a tailspin before it crashed.

Returning to the Orel camp after finishing a service, Lieutenant Ramón Luca de Tena y Laso saw a Russian aircraft being attacked by Captain Alós and Lieutenant Guibert, so he joined them in the attack. Upon receiving the new arrival's shots, the Russian began to shed pieces of its wing and leak oil. The lieutenant gave it two more passes, and, on the last one, the enemy plane was shot down. And so ended a great day for the Spanish fighters.

The next day, which had bad weather severely restrict activity, the German Spaniards at the Orel field were surprised to see an American-made Bell P-39 Airacobra aircraft circling over the runway at 11:00 with the intention of landing, which it then did. The Russian pilot then opened the cockpit and began to ask what forces were garrisoning the airfield, thinking that it was already in Russian hands or because he was completely lost. At that point, he was fired upon from several places, so he took off without hesitation, heading toward his lines.

Ensign Aldecoa with the Iron Cross he obtained after his combats against Soviet aircraft. After finishing his period of service with the 3rd and 4th Squadrons (to the latter of which he was temporarily attached), he managed to shoot down seven aircraft.

This Bf 109 E-3 ('1' white) was used by the Spanish pilots of the 1st Squadron during their training at the Werneuchen Fighter School. The yellow-painted engine cowling and fairing can be seen. The aircraft had no Spanish insignia, as it did not belong to the 1st Squadron but to the Fighter School. (Courtesy of José Fernández/Teodor Liviu Morosanu (henceforth 'JF/TLM'))

Bf 109 E-4 belonging to the 1st Squadron during the autumn of 1941. As was normal for *Luftwaffe* aircraft on the Eastern Front, the aircraft has a yellow-painted band around the fuselage, on the nose and under the wingtips. On the port side of the nose is the insignia of the 1st Squadron. (JF/TLM)

Bf 109 E-7/B ('M' black) belonging to the 1st Blue Squadron, known in the *Luftwaffe* as '15.(Span)/JG 27', Staritza airfield, November 1941. The aircraft has the yellow identification colour on the nose and fuselage band, as well as the Spanish unit insignia on the nose. This aircraft was flown by Commander Ángel Salas Larrazabal and, at that time, had already shot down six enemy aircraft, as indicated by the victory marks painted on its tail. The black triangle with a white border near the cross on the fuselage was the mark of ground attack units in the *Luftwaffe* (*Schlachtflieger*). (Courtesy of Claes Sundin (henceforth 'CS'))

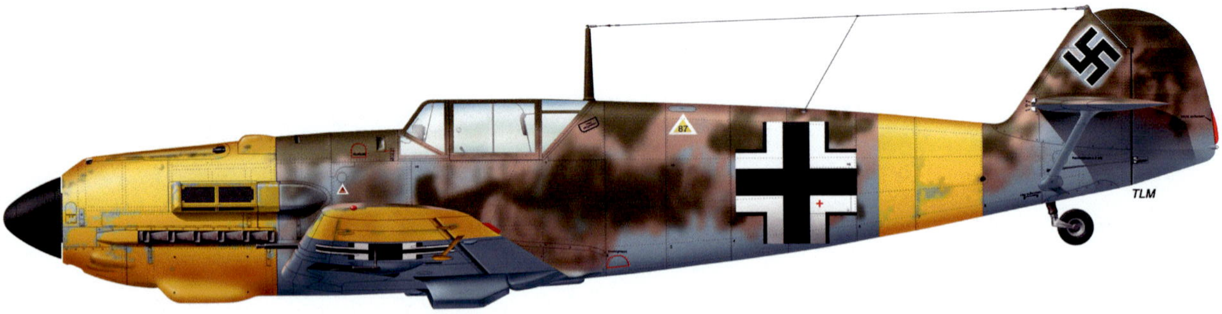

This aircraft was the only Bf 109 E-4 tropicalised version used by the 1st Blue Squadron, autumn 1941. It has no additional armour on the front of the cockpit and no Spanish insignia. (JF/TLM)

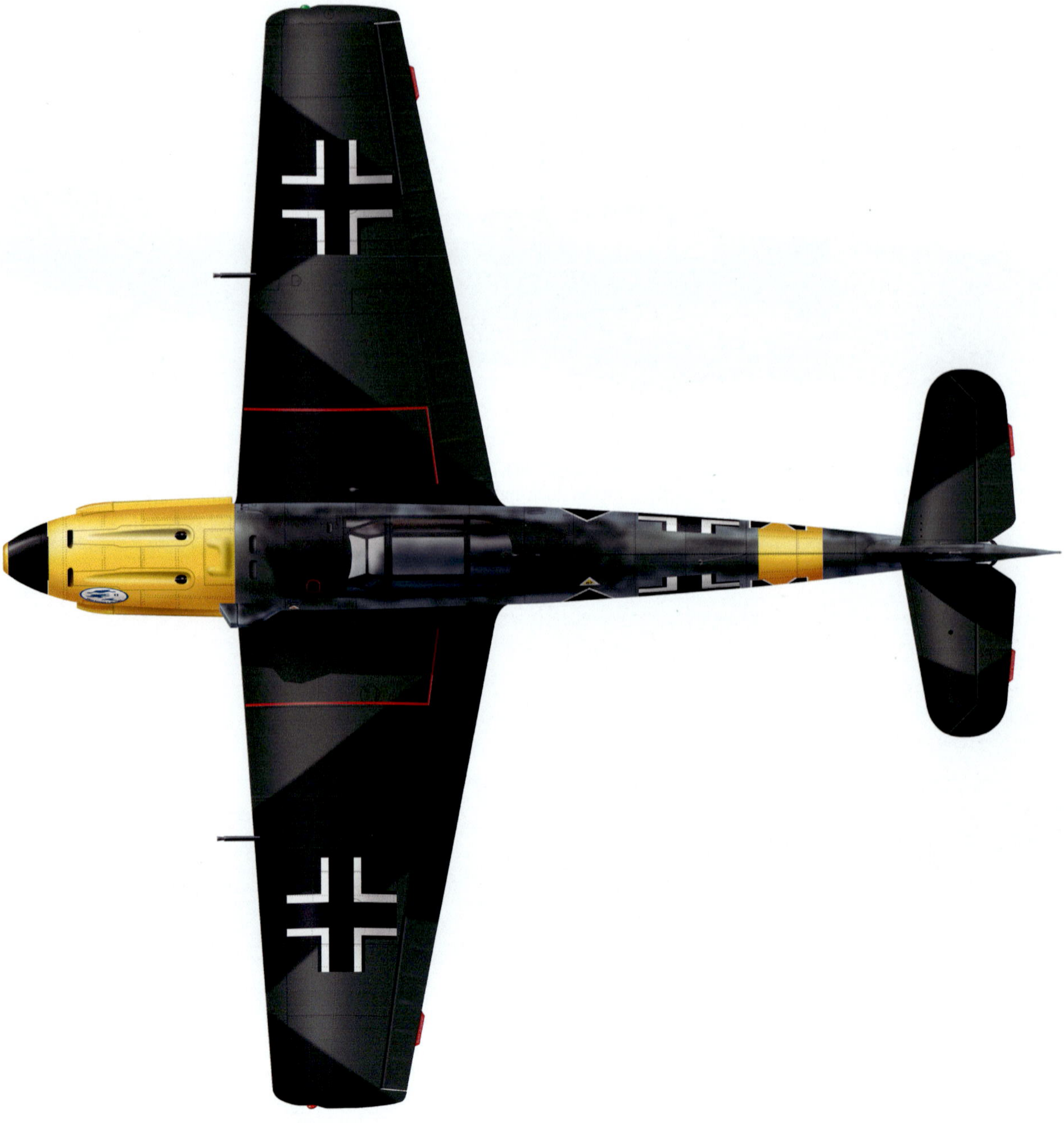

Top view of a Bf 109 E-4 of the 1st Squadron, where the camouflage used on the aircraft can be seen. (JF/TLM)

Bottom view of a Bf 109 E-4 of the 1st Squadron, where the camouflage used on the aircraft can be seen. (JF/TLM)

The Bf 109 F-2 (SG+YQ) was one of the aircraft used by the pilots of the 2nd Blue Squadron during their training at the Werneuchen Fighter School. The aircraft does not carry any Spanish insignia. (JF/TLM)

Bf 109 F-2 ('1' black) belonging to the 2nd Blue Squadron, known in the *Luftwaffe* as '15.(Span)/JG 51', Orel airfield, August 1942. This aircraft, usually flown by Lieutenant Andrés Robles Cebrián, bears the unit's insignia on the port side of the nose and the Falangist symbol of the 'yoke and arrows' between the cross and the yellow band on the fuselage. (CS)

Top view of a Bf 109 F-2 of the 2nd Squadron, where the camouflage used on the aircraft can be seen. (JF/TLM)

Bottom view of a Bf 109 F-2 of the 2nd Squadron, where the camouflage used on the aircraft can be seen. (JF/TLM)

Bf 109 F-2 ('7' black) Werk N.5423 belonging to the 2nd Blue Squadron, Orel airfield, August 1942. The aircraft has the Falangist symbol of the 'yoke and arrows' between the cross and the yellow band on the fuselage. The text painted in black on the starboard side of the engine cowling reads, '*CABO MECÁNICO ZARO ¡Presente!*' (CORPORAL MECHANIC ZARO Present!), as a tribute to one of the mechanics killed in service of the unit. (CS)

Bf 109 F-2 ('7' black) Werk N.5423 belonging to the 2nd Blue Squadron, Orel airfield, August 1942. (JF/TLM)

After the death of Captain Noriega Labat, one of the aircraft of the 2nd Squadron (the black Bf 109 F-2 No. 1) had the phrase '*CAPITÁN NORIEGA ¡Presente!*' (CAPTAIN NORIEGA Present!) painted on its starboard engine cowling as a tribute to the pilot. (JF/TLM)

This Bf 109 F-2 ('13' black) was the aircraft used by 2nd Squadron Inspector Commander Julio Salvador Díaz-Benjumea. Although not visible, as on many of the aircraft of the 2nd Squadron, the unit's emblem was painted on the port side of the engine cowling. (JF/TLM)

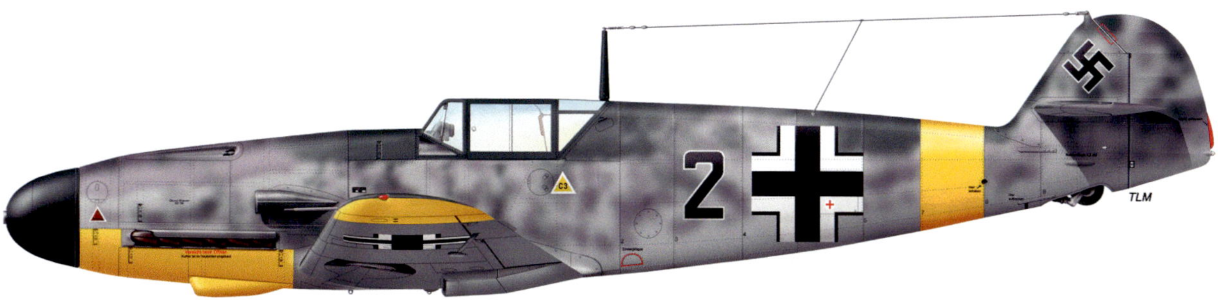

Bf 109 F-2 ('2' black) belonging to the 2nd Blue Squadron, Orel airfield, autumn 1942. Gradually, the aircraft of the Spanish unit were used without the unit insignia painted on the port side of the engine cowling. (JF/TLM)

This Bf 109 F-2 ('3' black) is another example of how, on many occasions, the aircraft of the 2nd Squadron, lacking Spanish insignia, were similar to those used by German *Luftwaffe* pilots. (JF/TLM)

Bf 109 F-2 ('4' black) of the 2nd Blue Squadron, Orel airfield, September 1942. The aircraft only has the insignia typical of all *Luftwaffe* aircraft on the Eastern Front. (JF/TLM)

Bf 109 F-2 ('11' black) of the 2nd Blue Squadron with the typical winter camouflage used by *Luftwaffe* aircraft, where the emblem of the Spanish unit stands out. This aircraft was flown by Lieutenant Barañano on 13 October 1942 and managed to shoot down an Il-2. (JF/TLM)

On this occasion (the black Bf 109 F-2 No. 12), the winter white paint did not respect the 2nd Squadron's insignia, Orel airfield, winter 1942. (JF/TLM)

Bf 109 F-2 ('10' black) before being painted with winter camouflage at the Orel airfield in July 1942. The aircraft shows no differences in the camouflage used compared to other *Luftwaffe* aircraft on the Eastern Front. (JF/TLM)

When the cold Russian winter arrived, the 2nd Squadron aircraft were painted in washable white over their original camouflage, as can be seen in the picture of this Bf 109 F-2 ('16' black) of the 2nd Squadron, completely painted white after the winter camouflage had been applied. This aircraft was photographed in January 1943 at the Orel airfield when it was already assigned to the 3rd Blue Squadron. (JF/TLM)

Bf 109 F-2 ('2' black), Orel airfield, December 1942. In this case, the squadron insignia painted on the engine was respected and retained. This aircraft was also flown by pilots of the 3rd Squadron, who, replacing the 2nd Squadron, kept their aircraft. (JF/TLM)

Fw 190 A-3 belonging to the 3rd Blue Squadron, known in the *Luftwaffe* as '15.(Span)/JG 51', Orel airfield, June 1943. The white No. 5 was flown by Captain Gonzalo Hevia. The arrival of this new model of aircraft coincided with the peak of the Spanish unit's aerial combat activity. The aircraft carries no Spanish insignia, and only the yellow markings used on the Eastern Front stand out under the engine, on the wingtips and the fuselage bands. (CS)

The white Fw 190 A-3 No. 24 of the 3rd Blue Squadron while flying in the Orel sector at the Orel airfield during the spring of 1943. The Spanish Fw 190s never had their squadron insignia painted on the engine. This aircraft, flown by Ensign Aldecoa (already flying attached to the 4th Squadron), received multiple hits from Soviet anti-aircraft artillery on 6 August 1943. (JF/TLM)

The white Fw 190 A-2 No. 5 of the 4th Blue Squadron painted in winter camouflage at the Orel airfield at the beginning of 1944. The Spanish Fw 190s were of the A-2 and A-3 models, while those used by the Germans during the same period were already the A-4 and A-5 models. (JF/TLM)

The same white Fw 190 A-2 No. 5, now in summer camouflage, Orel airfield, August 1943. It was flown by Ensign Chicharro Lamamié de Clairac and shot down on 21 August 1943 when it hit a LaGG-5 near Nikolskoje. (JF/TLM)

Fw 190 A-4 belonging to the 4th Blue Squadron, known in the *Luftwaffe* as '15.(Span)/JG 51', Seschtschinskaja airfield, October 1943. The white No. 11 was flown by Lieutenant José Cavanilles, who, until his downing on 10 January 1944, achieved four victories against the enemy. (CS)

The white Fw 190 A-2 No. 12 was another aircraft flown by Lieutenant José Cavanilles (also known as '*Pepín*' Cavanilles). The aircraft has the camouflage normally used in that period on the Eastern Front (Smolensk airfield, September 1943). The brave pilot was shot down and killed south-east of the village of Cawydowitschi on 10 January 1944. (JF/TLM)

Another aircraft of the 4th Squadron was the white Fw 190 A-2 No. 22, flown by Lieutenant Francisco Valiente Zárraga. (JF/TLM)

The camouflage usually used on the Eastern Front by the aircraft of the 4th Squadron was the same as that used by the aircraft of JG 51, to which the Spaniards belonged. Pictured is the white No. 18 at the Seschtschinskaja airfield in October 1943. (JF/TLM)

The 5th Blue Squadron exchanged the Fw 190s used by the 4th Squadron for modern Bf 109 G-6s like the white No.2 pictured here at the Bobruisk airfield in February 1944. The service period of this unit was limited between February and March 1944, so the camouflage used was typical of the winter period. (JF/TLM)

1st Blue Squadron Deployment (15.(Spanische)/ JG27). Deployment and movement during the Winter soviet counteroffensive.

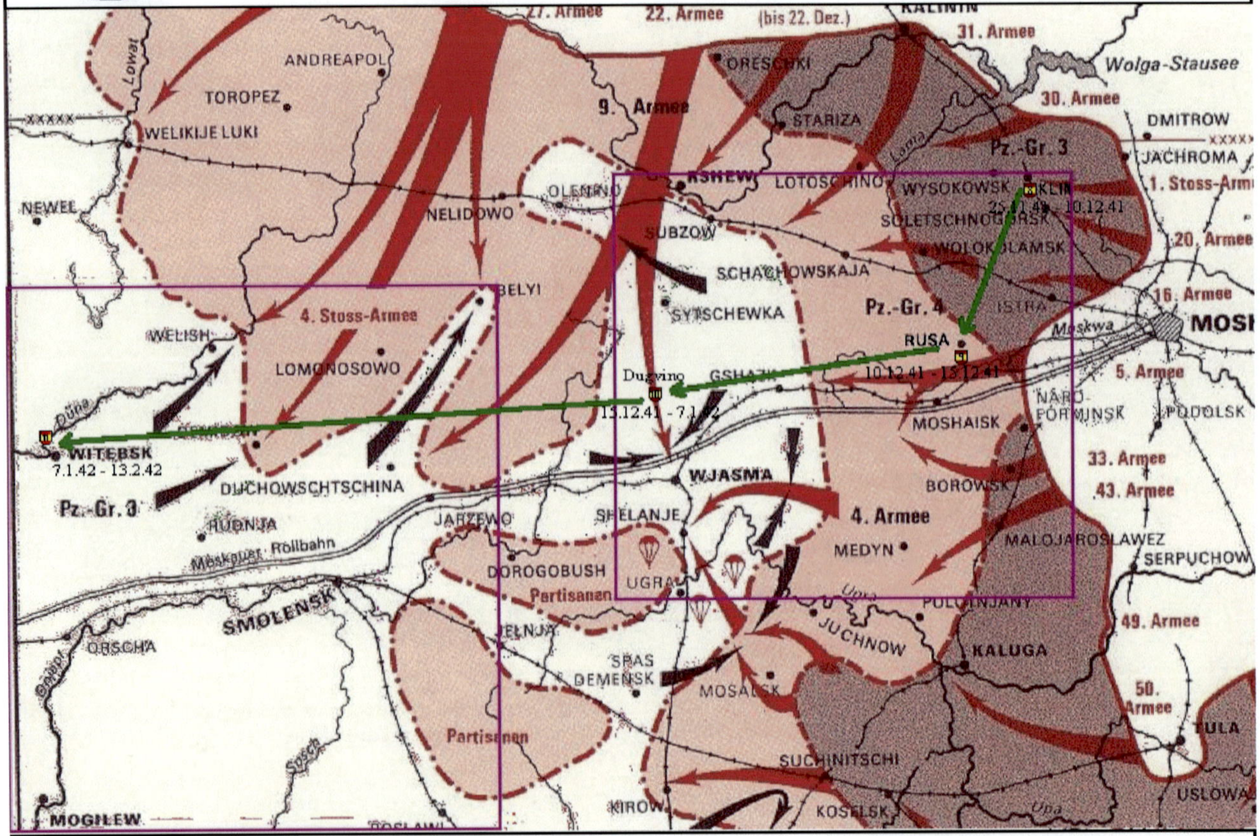

Front lines:

- Front line at 5/6 December 1942
- Front line at 1st January 1942
- Front line at late April 1942
- Soviet Counteroffensive lines.
- Soviet parachutist dropping during 18-24 January, 1942.
- German counteroffensive lines.
- Blue Squadron movements.
- Base location (in numbers you can know the order)

1st Blue Squadron Deployment (15.(Spanische)/JG27). Deployment and movement during the Operation "Taifun" (Typhoon) and road to Moscow.

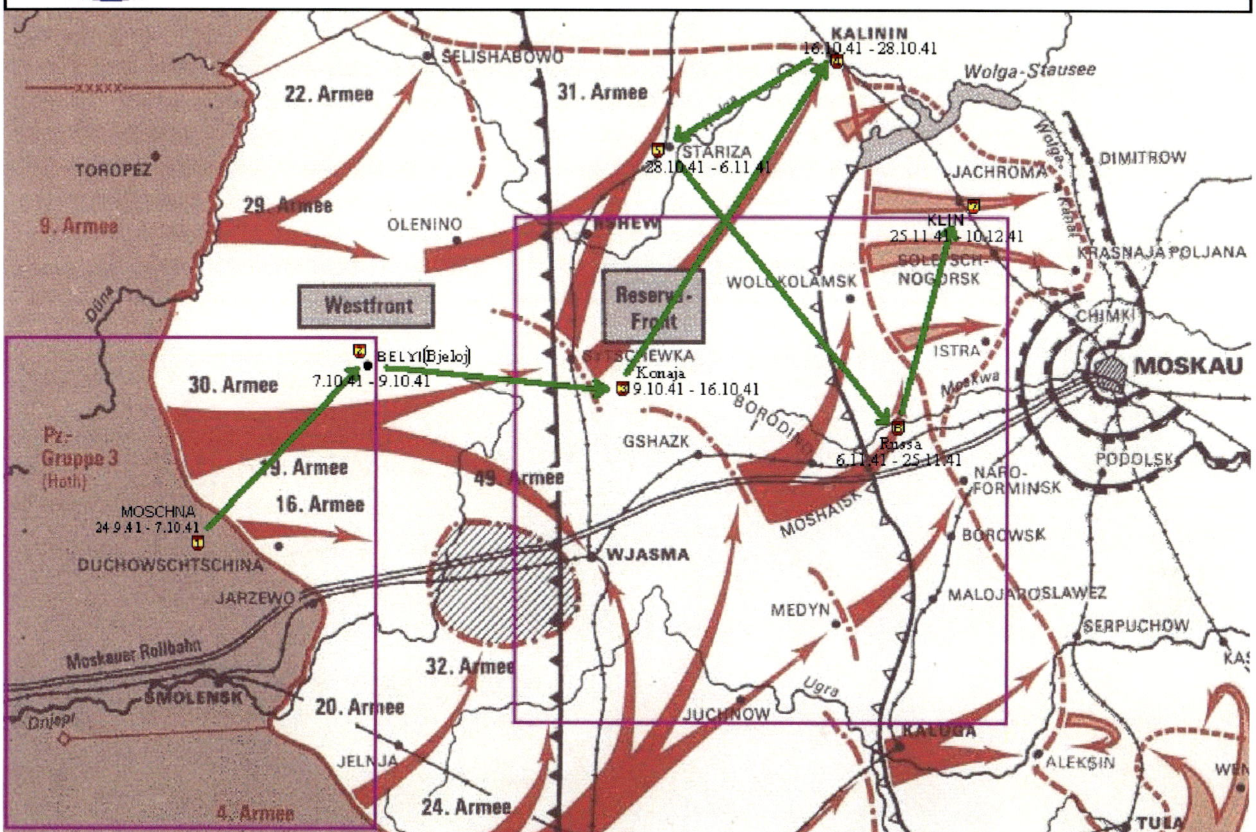

Front lines:

- Front line at 30th September, 1941.
- Offensive from 30th September to 30th October 1941.
- Front line at 10th October, 1941.
- Front Line from 30th October to 15th November.
- Offensive from 15th November, 1941 to 5th December 1942.
- Front line at 5th December, 1942.

- Blue Squadron movements.
- Base location (in numbers you can know the order)

2nd Blue Squadron Deployment (15.(Spanische)/JG51). Deployment from 8th June to 30th November 1942.

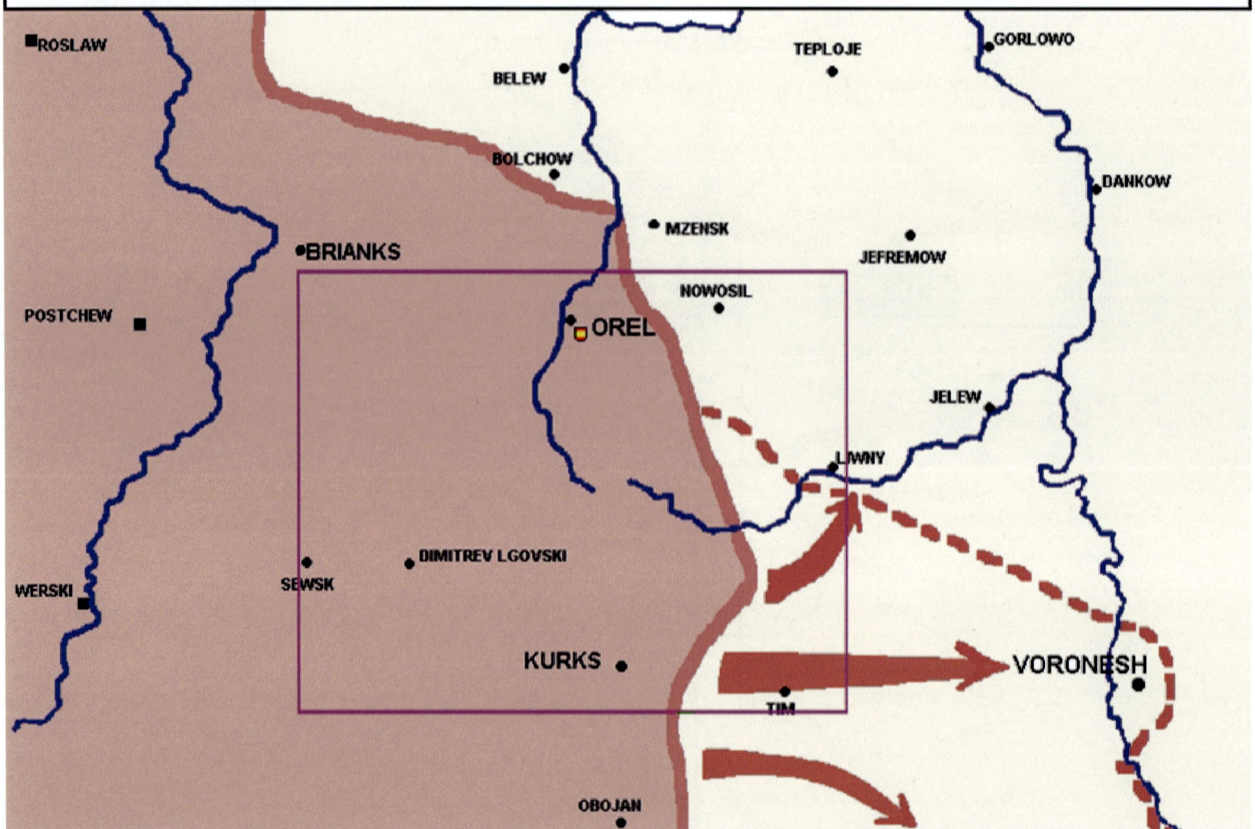

Front lines:

- Front line at 28th June, 1942.
- German offensive: Operation Blue
- Front Line at 7th July, 1942
- Base location

The uncertainty provided by the advance of the Red Army (occupying Rzhev on 3 March and Viazma on 12 March) led the Spanish squadron to receive the order on 1 March to move to the base at Seschtschinskaja, located between Orel and Smolensk, to support the German withdrawal in the Rzhev area more easily. The transfer took place in the beginning of March: some of the pilots (including Major Ferrándiz) in their planes and the specialists in Ju 52s. On 2 March, in four Ju 52s, most of the specialists left for the new camp, and, a little later, the rest of the pilots left in their Bf 109 F-2s. However, the weather worsened, and Captain Alós was forced to land in Bryansk. Captain Gavilán and Lieutenants Azqueta and Calleja were forced to fly close together and almost at ground level, but they still managed to land at Seschtschinskaja. Under the command of Lieutenant Larraz, the rest of the ground crew left Orel in a column of trucks.

Result of the Russian bombing of the Seschtschinskaja field on the night of 17–18 March 1943. The growing Soviet air superiority was beginning to show with the numerous attacks on *Luftwaffe* airfields.

The new sector assigned to the Spaniards covered a line from Spas-Demensk in the north-west, situated on the railway line from Smolensk to Ssuchinitschi and Moscow, to Shisdra and continuing from north-north-west to south-south-east, with a pronounced enemy incoming at Kirow. On 3 March, the squadron was already in Seschtschinskaja, and the first thing the pilots did was the usual flights to familiarise themselves with the area and search for air navigation landmarks to return to their airfield: a north–south railway from Wjasma to Bryansk and two lakes, one at Kirow and one at Ludinowo, that were visible from a great distance.

In this sector assigned to the 3rd Squadron was a large area dominated by partisans from south of Ludinowo to its north-western part. To the south, there was another larger area a few kilometres from the base, which was also occupied by partisans, who were supplied during the night by Russian aircraft that sometimes landed in these areas. From these areas, the Soviet's low-flying attacks were channelled, which often caused the alarm pair to take off after they had already begun to bomb and strafe the camp.

On 5–6 March, a few missions were flown without incident. This was not the case on 7 March: the day had barely begun to dawn when the Bf 109s took off for a free fighter mission over the Shisdra area, at the same time protecting a group of He 111s.

During the patrol of the front, Major Ferrándiz, who had Lieutenant Azqueta as wingman, saw five aircraft that he identified as Yak-1s, although with the doubt that they might be Hurricanes instead since it was the first time he had seen this type of aircraft. The commander climbed up, and, with the sun at his back, he positioned himself behind and below the tail of one of them, shot at it and, with a second burst, set it on fire and shot it down. But the combat continued, and

The LaGG-3 was the Soviet aircraft type that the Spanish pilots shot down more frequently (mainly 3rd and 4th Squadrons). The tally for the Spanish pilots was 58 LaGG-3s. (Public Domain)

the second pair, made up of Captain Gavilán (No.5) and Lieutenant Alejandro Pérez González, launched themselves into the attack. Gavilán recalled of this combat:

> I saw a ball of fighters fighting and I jumped on one of them. We crossed each other's noses and almost collided, that pilot knew what he was doing. I had such a hard time catching his tail that when I got him and started shooting at him, I realised that the cannon had jammed, forcing me to get even closer to hit him with the machine guns. I blinded myself too much, I flicked left to get out, but it was too late; I cut his depth rudder like cheese with my left plane and he went into a tailspin. My plane hit a spin, which I managed to pull out because I was high. I immediately thought of jumping, but when I saw that 'that thing', despite the vibrations, was flying, I gave up; as I was over enemy territory. My first intention was to get to our lines and land in a field, but once there I told myself that I might make it to the base. I had to fly the plane by helping myself with my leg to hold the stick, the pitot tube had disappeared and, of course, I had no indication of speed. At our airfield in Seschtschinskaja, the thaw had started, but at night it was still cold and the field looked icy. I did not dare to fly at low speed, for fear of going into a tailspin, and the flaps were inoperative; so I landed at about 200 km/h and waited for it to stop, which it did. When I got out and saw that about two metres of the left plane were shredded, I realised that the Messerschmitt was flying very well. Incidentally, I was never sure whether the plane I shot down was a Yak or a Hurricane.[3]

The following day, under the command of Major Ferrándiz, they began their services, which as usual were bomber escort and free fighter missions. The first was to protect *Stukas* in the Shisdra sector, which passed without incident. As there was enough fuel left, they decided that they could at least do a free fighter mission, during which they observed eight Il-2s flying close to the ground in an irregular formation. The Russians spotted them and moved into defensive formation. On the second pass, Major Ferrándiz managed to get behind and a little lower than one of them and fired all the ammunition he had left in his cannon at it, but he did not see it fall, which upset him considerably since he could

3 Arráez Cerdá, 'Les Espagnols de la Luftwaffe', 18, pp.63–64.

not confirm victory. Fortunately, one of the observation posts in the village of Ljudinowo, on the same front line, had witnessed and reported it.

In the afternoon, the Iron Cross 2nd Class was awarded to deserving personnel, and there was a fitting celebration with 'free quartermastering', although with the advice not to overdo it since services would resume within a few hours.

On 9 March, the 3rd Squadron's successes continued as two more victories were achieved. They happened during a free fighter mission when two LaGG-5s crossed over the Spaniards at a higher altitude. Lieutenant Rafael Calleja González-Camino launched himself in pursuit, catching up with them and firing on one with his machine guns. The other LaGG-5 veered towards him, so he started to turn and, from a little lower down, fired a burst that hit it squarely, knocking it down. Captain Antonio Alós headed for the other LaGG-5 and shot it down on his third pass. It crashed some 30km north of Shisdra, its wings shredded and fuselage split at the cockpit.

The following day, only free fighter services were carried out. During one of them, Captain Gavilán saw an Il-2 flying behind him at low altitude, so he began his attack, hitting it with his first shots and seeing how he took a leg out of its landing gear. He then positioned himself behind its tail and fired at it until it went into a dive and crashed. Captain Alós saw seven Il-2s flying at cloud cover height (about 200m) and accompanied by five LaGG-5s, so he managed to get behind the tail of one of the LaGG-5s. Lacking cannon ammunition, he fired three bursts of machine-gun fire and hit it in the engine, which began to smoke black and burn before crashing to the ground.

Captain Gavilán of the 3rd Blue Squadron poses contentedly with his Bf 109 F, showing its shattered left wing after the fighting on 7 March 1943. He managed to shoot down nine soviet planes.

The pair formed by Lieutenant Narciso García García '*El Terete*' and Ensign Alfonso Teixidor '*El Retaco*' were also involved. Teixidor recalled about their first combat:

> We saw a formation of seven single-seat Il-2s. According to procedure '*El Terete*' attacked while I protected him and when he ran out of 20mm ammunition, the only option against these flying battleships, he ordered me to attack and he went to protect me. The Il-2 went down to protect itself with ground cover, but I found a hole and went in deeper. I fired and hit it in the engine and radiator, watching the propeller stop dead and one leg of the gear deploy on its own. It dived into a nearby field for a crash landing. We stayed above it until the pilot abandoned the aircraft, at which point, as required, because it was in an enemy zone, we strafed the aircraft to render it completely useless. On the final pass the pilot bade us farewell with an impeccable arm in the air.[4]

4 Arráez Cerdá, 'Les Espagnols de la Luftwaffe', 18, pp.64–65.

On 11–12 March, the usual escort and free fighter services were carried out without incident. At this time, the Russian pilots fighting the Spaniards seemed to be very inexperienced. They flew in odd-numbered formations, unlike the Germans, and had few tactics of their own. One of them was to place one plane very low, with two others protecting it overhead. Certainly, the best Russian units did not fly in the Spanish sector. This would change months later, as the Soviets would send their best pilots against the Spanish.

On 13 March, the free fighter services were carried out in the Uljanovo area. While returning from that area, Captain Hevia and Lieutenant Pérez-Muñoz received a warning of enemy aircraft and quickly headed for the area where they had been sighted. Captain Hevia positioned himself behind the aircraft on the left of the formation, but another Russian swerved with the intention of getting behind Hevia's aircraft. The lieutenant saw this and took advantage of the situation to get behind the Russian and successfully shoot him down. He then gave a jerk and saw another LaGG-3 starting to flee, so he accelerated. The Soviet noticed him and tried to hide in the clouds before Pérez-Muñoz opened fire, shooting him down. Captain Hevia fired on his LaGG-3, which also tried to escape towards its lines but was shot down.

As for Lieutenant Juan Roselló Simonet, he was attacked by three LaGG-3s flying higher up. When he became aware of them, he made a violent turn that allowed him to get on the tail of one of those trying to surprise him. At about 80m, he fired with his machine guns and cannon, shooting it down.

14 March dawned clear, and so the 3rd Squadron's services were constant with all available aircraft. In one of them, Ensign Teixidor had a mishap and almost fell prisoner:

> I was flying alongside Vara de Rey, on a mission to escort an Fw 189 and with communications failures in my aircraft. I noticed what could have been an anti-aircraft impact or an engine explosion, which began to crackle, making it impossible to read the instruments. I was forced to stop the engine and glide to a clearing in the forest, which was close to a railway track (which in principle were all controlled by the Germans). Just before touching down I spotted an armed patrol that might have been partisans, so as soon as I set foot on the ground I ran across an icy riverbed to avoid tracks in the snow, in breach of our orders to destroy the aircraft to prevent its seizure by the enemy. I ran for about a couple of hours (listening to my pursuers and the barking of dogs) until exhaustion prevented me from continuing. I crouched in a thicket and waited with my gun mounted until I heard German being spoken, whereupon I made myself known as a pilot of the Spanish squadron; I understood them in French, because the patrol leader was Alsatian. He explained that, just as I had mistaken them for partisans, whose pursuit was precisely the mission of the patrol, they had taken me for a Russian. They could not take me to Divisional Headquarters, which was 30 km to the north, so they assigned me a Russian prisoner and a sledge. Their recommendations were blunt: take the compass and the gun and have him take you to our command post; if he strays, kill him. In this bizarre way I began my march; I managed to get there, but not without some hardships, for when we crossed an icy river, our sledge sank and we had to pull it out between the two of us, getting up to our waists in the freezing water. To get to the base I had to travel along the front in a convoy of lorries picking up the wounded; then in trains that only ran at night, because during the day they were attacked by Russian bombers. When I arrived, the base had been brutally bombed by aircraft, my room had been destroyed and, what was more serious, as soon as I entered the Pavilion I found myself in front of the *chapelle ardente* [burning chapel] of '*El Terete*', who had been killed in action [KIA].[5]

The number of Soviet aircraft flying in the area where the Spanish were had greatly increased and posed a great risk to the air base. Thus, almost at dusk on 14 March, Soviet aircraft of the DB-3 and TB-3 type attacked the Orel field intensively, being met by their flak, which at least managed to shoot down one DB-3. Several of the buildings were destroyed. German personnel casualties were heavy, although the Spanish suffered only a few wounded and the death of Private Jiménez Martínez, who was the first casualty of the 3rd Squadron. When everything seemed to have calmed down, the Russians bombed again at 23:00 for 20 minutes, although on this occasion the damage suffered was minor. Private Jiménez Martínez was buried in the base cemetery on 15 March during a break between bombing raids, receiving the corresponding military honours. In these bombardments, some of the planes were all but destroyed, and one was totally destroyed, the mechanics working hard to put them back together again as quickly as possible.

From 15 to 17 March, the Russian bombardment of the airfield continued, causing new destruction and casualties among the Germans but no Spanish casualties.

On 18 March, Lieutenant Narciso García '*El Terete*' took off at 14:00 to carry out a test flight in one of the *Zacutos* that had just been repaired. He took off without any problems, but, when making a sharp turn after about 20 minutes of flight, he entered a steep dive and crashed, without managing to parachute out. His mechanic had been terrified to see something detach from the plane. Upon investigation, it was found that the fixed tailplane was open at the leading edge and 500m from the aircraft.

5 Arráez Cerdá, 'Les Espagnols de la Luftwaffe', 18, pp.65–66.

At 01:00 on 19 March, the airfield where the Spaniards were stationed was again attacked by Soviet bombers, but, as soon as the first rays of sunlight appeared, services still began. In one of them, Captain Gavilán and Lieutenant Roselló were attacked by three LaGG-3s, but they dodged them easily, and Gavilán dived after one of them, giving it a tail pass. He saw through the tracers how he hit the LaGG-3, which, at ground level and with full engine power, managed to get into their lines. Since the bombing was almost continuous, the order was given for the specialist and troop personnel, with the exception of those on duty, to move at 17:00 to some schools near the camp.

At 04:00 on 20 March, the ground crews were already at the airfield, as the missions began at the first light of the day, with free fighter over Shisdra and protection of the *Stukas* in the Spatember area.

At 10:00, in a moving ceremony, honours were paid to Lieutenant Narciso García '*El Terete*', and his remains were laid to rest in the base cemetery.

Emotional funeral of one of the 3rd Squadron's men, attended by the inspector commander of the Spanish unit, Major Ferrándiz.

On 21 March, the Spaniards suffered the loss of Captain José Antonio García-Alfonso Menéndez-Conde, who was shot down flying Bf 109 F-2 No.19. According to the report made by Lieutenant Bernardo Meneses Orozco, his partner on the mission:

> We took off very early, at 05:45 with a mission to protect the bombing of the Heinkel He 111. Upon arriving at Spas-Demensk I told the captain that I noticed something strange about my plane. He asked me if I could take the Heinkel He 111 bombing and I said yes. We were flying to the right of the bombers and, a little farther back, when I saw to my left, at a distance of 300 metres, several Russian aircraft, of the LaGG-5 type, coming in to attack the bombers, I radioed the captain, and we both headed towards them. I tried to attack one, but it gave a jerk and stayed higher. The captain passed me on my right and reversed, telling me over the radio to be careful. A second aircraft was behind me and I was following the first one, which came ahead of me in the turn. The captain kept telling me over the radio to be careful, until I stopped hearing him. I started calling out to him but got no answer. Finding myself alone, I turned back to the field, where I landed at 07:00. The crew of the He 111 reported that they had seen a German aircraft fall on fire.[6]

6 Arráez Cerdá, 'Les Espagnols de la Luftwaffe', 18, p.66.

On 22 March, a communication was received that the body of Captain Menéndez-Conde had been found in Privetok, in the Spas-Demensk area, near the Moscow road and next to some trenches. Brigadier Basanta was ordered to leave with an interpreter and a soldier to collect the remains of the captain, which he did the following day. In his *DIARIO DE CAMPAÑA DE LA 3ª ESCUADRILLA EXPEDICIONARIA* (*CAMPAIGN DIARY OF THE 3RD EXPEDITIONARY SQUAD*), Brigadier Alberto Martínez Basanta wrote:

> At 05:00 we left in a lorry to try to recover the body of Captain Menéndez-Conde. From Spas-Demensk, which was under Russian artillery fire, we drove along tank tracks to the point where the captain was. The completely wrecked aircraft lay next to an Isba, embedded in a funnel about two metres deep, which it produced upon reaching the ground; the captain, whose head was missing, perhaps because of a cannon shot from the plane that attacked him, lay about ten metres from the aircraft, with no mutilations to be seen, although his left side, from halfway up, was scorched. Due to the effect of the low temperature, the body was stuck to the ground.
>
> Once recognized and collected, the return began; at 16:00, the Germans tried to stop the lorry because road traffic was not allowed after that time, due to the guerrilla attacks, but having obtained authorisation, not without first assuming full responsibility, the journey continued, arriving at the camp at 19:30, at the moment when the Russian planes were bombing the base, a bombardment that lasted until 22:00.[7]

On 24 March, an alarm was received, and the service pair took off, returning without having encountered any enemy in the air. At 14:00, the squadron formed to pay posthumous tribute to Captain Menéndez-Conde, who was buried in the base cemetery alongside his comrades. The atmosphere among the Spaniards was desolate, as in less than a week they had lost two pilots and an excellent soldier. The squadron had also lost several aircraft, destroyed or damaged, due to persistent Russian bombing, and, as if that were not enough, those that had remained intact were very worn out since they had not been able to undergo a general overhaul and were already well used upon arrival, both by the 2nd Squadron and by the *Luftwaffe Staffeln* from which they came.

In the following days, the temperature improved, and the services went on without incident, except on 26 March when 16 Pe-2 planes bombed the camp, although fortunately without aiming since the bombs fell far away.

On 28 March, when everyone thought that the snow was over, it snowed at dawn. But the most important thing was the order that Captain Gonzalo Hevia, the squadron's top ace who spoke perfect German, was sent to Smolensk, where JG 51's General Staff was based, to be attached to the staff in order to fly and get to know the Focke Wulf Fw 190 A-2, the aircraft with which the 3rd Squadron was to be refitted. A group of specialists made up of Sergeants Costea and Saponi, three lance corporals and six corporals went with him to study the maintenance of this type of aircraft.

As mentioned, the aircraft flown by the Spaniards were heavily used, as some Bf 109s had been handed over by the 2nd Squadron pilots to the 3rd Squadron, requiring continuous maintenance to keep them flying, and some others had been destroyed by Soviet attacks. In addition, Soviet bombing had caused damage to aircraft at the Seschtschinskaja base, so there was an urgent need to obtain new aircraft for the Spanish. The aircraft of choice were the Fw 190 A-2 and A-3.

The Fw 190 was a magnificent aircraft but one that the Spanish pilots had not received any training for. The training the pilots received was to fly the Bf 109, and Spain did not have this newer type of aircraft in the EdA. It was considered whether to retrain the whole squadron with the new aircraft or to send a Spanish pilot with several mechanics to Smolensk so that they could learn everything they needed to fly and maintain the aircraft in operation. The second option was chosen, and so, at the end of March, Captain Hevia and a group of mechanics from the squadron went to Smolensk to learn about their next aircraft, the Fw 190. Captain Hevia was not chosen at random but for two important reasons: he was a great pilot, as demonstrated by his aerial victories, and he also spoke German.

It is not the purpose of this text to consider the Bf 109 superior to the Fw 190 or the other way around, but what is true is that they were aircraft with many structural differences and variations in the way they were flown. The important thing is that the new aircraft that the 3rd Squadron pilots received enabled the Spanish victories in Russian skies to continue.

The month of March was coming to an end, and the performance of the Spanish proved to be very good, as they had shot down many enemy aircraft, but the number of squadron casualties was rising. The impression of the Spanish pilots was that the Russian pilots were not all experts, and there were many occasions in which they behaved like novices, making the Spaniards' job easier.

On 1 April, Captain Hevia became the first Spanish pilot to fly the Fw 190 A-2. After receiving a quick ground instruction, he climbed into his new fighter, which had No.8 painted on its fuselage. He was briefed by the mechanic, got into the cockpit, which was much larger than that of the Messerschmitt, adjusted his parachute and harnesses and checked the oxygen. He then pressed the start button, and the BMW 801 engine began to roar. After the final checks, he took off

7 Arráez Cerdá, 'Les Espagnols de la Luftwaffe', 18, p.66.

These four 3rd Squadron pilots chat before leaving for the next mission with one of their Fw 190 A-3s.

at 180km/h. After 45 minutes of flight, with three takes and in the air, Captain Hevia made a stupendous three-point landing and was highly satisfied with such a fine aircraft.

Bad weather prevented Hevia from requesting any flights in the following days. On 4 April, he first flew 25 minutes in training and then went out again for his first war service as part of the JG 51 General Staff, which may well have been his last. According to his memories:

> We were about to perform a free fighter service with four Fw 190s. When we were ready to take off, one of the planes was forced to return to the line due to a breakdown. We took off with the remaining three; this type of formation was typical of Soviet aircraft, as we always took off in even formations. We came across another formation of Fw 190s and one of them dropped down and got on my tail, I did not react, as I thought that this 'comrade' wanted to salute me. But what was my surprise when I saw the tracers passing me from all sides; one impact took out the undercarriage and disabled the flap. When he overtook me and recognised the German emblems, that pilot went to pieces. The engine had not been touched and, wounded in one hand, I prepared to land; I could not get the flap out, but a cannon shot had disabled my tail wheel, leaving a lump of iron that helped me to slow the plane down. A short time later, *Feldwebel* Mildner landed, totally discomposed and apologetic. The squadron captain gave me the choice of the type of penalty, but I thought that the man had enough to deal with, although I jokingly decided that he should be penalised for firing so badly.[8]

Meanwhile, in Orel, the bad weather continued to prevail, resulting in very few services, which was to be welcomed given the exhaustion suffered by the Bf 109 F-2s.

On 7 April, the specialist personnel returned from Smolensk, and the Germans were impressed by their competence and speed of assimilation, for which they were congratulated by *Oberstleutnant* Nordmann.

Meanwhile, Captain Hevia continued to fly in the Smolensk field attached to the staff squadron on war services, arriving on 14 April, when he achieved the first victory by a Spanish pilot at the controls of an Fw 190. According to him:

8 Arráez Cerdá, 'Les Espagnols de la Luftwaffe', 18, p.67.

> It was a very nice service. We left Smolensk very early in the morning with four planes heading for Orel, landed there and, while refuelling the planes, we heard about the mission: a formation of twenty-five '*Stukas*' was going to bomb a railway station north of Kursk. Our task was to present ourselves a little earlier over the Kursk field, 'lift the fighter' and fight it, making it impossible for them to attack the '*Stukas*'. We arrived at the vertical of the field, at about 3,000 metres, at the very moment when a Pe-2 could fit it. When we sighted it, the Pe-2 was making a left turn, and towards which my patrol leader, *Feldwebel* Tanzer [this pilot reached the rank of *Leutnant* and 143 victories, being decorated with the Knight's Cross of the Iron Cross], went, I followed him protecting his tail. The Fw 190 had more ground to cover than the Pe-2, so I did not understand why Tanzer did not reduce his speed to that of the enemy in order to shoot better and with more time. When he opened fire, I could see that the tracers passed behind and underneath the Russian without doing him any damage, while at the same time 'eating' him and overtaking him on the way up. In view of this, I slowed my engine, tightened up the turn and went for him. At the right moment I opened fire and almost immediately the Pe-2 reversed the direction of the turn to the right and continued to turn harder and harder, until it went into a very open spin. I followed it for a while with my eyes until I considered that it was not going to make it and I looked for my comrades. Nobody, I was alone. Just in case there were any flies, I began to gain altitude, at the same time as I scanned the sky with my eyes, because they must have been there. Suddenly, as I looked back and down, I saw two Yak-1s coming towards me. They were flying in tight formation and coming in from the right. Strangely, I did not panic nor get nervous. I realised that they were coming up much lower than me, and waited. They both fired at the same time and without raising their noses, so I realised that their bursts were passing underneath me. Despite lagging behind, they were so close that I could see the Cross of Lorraine painted on the rudder. That was the Normandie-Niemen Squadron. We kept climbing, and they came to waste ammunition. When they got tired or ran out of ammunition, they turned to the field. With my height advantage, catching the straggler was a matter of a moment. I opened fire when I thought I had him in a very good position and could see the tracers going into the fuselage. I did not follow him with my eyes to the ground because the red low fuel light had come on and the best thing to do was to get out. As I was convinced that I was alone, I did not waste time looking for anyone and decided to return home. Passing over the field command post, I made two warp passes: one by the Pe-2 and one by the Yak-1. When I got out of the plane, *Feldwebel* Tanzer was waiting for me and, before I could open my mouth, he said: 'If you testify that I shot down the Pe-2, I will confirm the Yak-1.' And I thought I was alone![9]

In the following days, the squadron continued with missions when the weather permitted. Thus, it was not possible to fly from 15 to 20 April. However, during the last day, a new football match was held between the Germans and Spaniards. Among the Spaniards, pilots Pérez-Muñoz, Pérez González and Aldecoa, Quartermaster Lieutenant Rafael Soler and specialists Alberto Fernández Basanta, Manuel Otero and Ramón Aja stood out as good players. In the evening, the NCOs organised a wonderful dinner that the pilots attended without the interruption of a Russian plane dropping its bombs on the field.

On 21 April, the weather changed, and the services that the condition of the Bf 109 F-2s allowed were resumed. But the highlight of the day was the landing of the first three Fw 190 A-2s for the squadron, piloted by Captain Hevia and two German NCOs. The following day, the familiarisation flights with the three aircraft began, as well as their entertainment by the specialists. After dark, a PS-84 reconnaissance plane flew over the airfield. On 23 April, training continued with the Fw 190 A-2s, and, on 24 April, there was a succession of alarm services carried out by the Bf 109 F-2s.

Finally, on 25 April, the Fw 190 A-2s began free fighter services. The next day, the alarm sounded.

Because the terrain had hardened sufficiently after the thaw, *Luftwaffe* fighter units began deploying to fields closer to the front. As a result, *Mölders* HQ abandoned Smolensk. In order not to leave this airfield unguarded, it was decided to split the 3rd Squadron, or 15.(Span)/JG 51, into two echelons, one to continue at Seschtschinskaja and the other to be deployed to Smolensk. Therefore, on 30 April, Captain Hevia, Lieutenants Calleja, Pérez-Muñoz and Meneses and Ensigns Guibert and Aldecoa took off for Smolensk. Hevia was logically chosen to command them because of his perfect knowledge of German, as the '*Freya*' radar system was used there for the free fighter and alarm services.

The month of May began with reconnaissance of the front and free fighter from the Smolensk field, which passed without any noteworthy developments. Those at Seschtschinskaja went out on alarms and free fighters, and, at 11:00, the field was bombed by a Pe-2 reconnaissance plane. An hour later, Lieutenant Pérez González and Ensign Teixidor took off on alarms. Soon after, four LaGG-3s appeared and began to strafe the field, but the Spanish pair spotted them and went after them. Pérez González managed to hit one of them, which broke its rudder and caused it to immediately crash.

In the following days, alarm, protection and free fighter flights were made from the two airfields without incident. But on 5 May, at Seschtschinskaja, an unfortunate accident occurred. Around midday, Lieutenant Juan Roselló Simonet

9 Arráez Cerdá, 'Les Espagnols de la Luftwaffe', 18, p.68.

The first three Fw 190s arrived at the Seschtschinskaja airfield on 21 April 1943. The white No.24 pictured here was Ensign Aldecoa's aircraft, which was damaged after a mission on 6 August 1943 by Soviet anti-aircraft artillery.

started to take off with Fw 190 No.7, which had just left the workshops and was to be tested in a 20-minute flight. As he carried out the tests, he reported by radio and said that everything was going perfectly. His last message was 'altitude six thousand metres, engine OK, propeller pitch, pressures and temperatures normal'.[10] But within seconds of receiving this message, the personnel on the line heard a loud engine roar and watched in bewilderment as the Fw 190 came down in a vertical dive from about 5,000m, crashing into the same field. When they thought that the pilot was still inside, they saw a parachute in the air in the shape of a sleeve from which Lieutenant Roselló was hanging, desperately trying to get it to open completely, which did not happen. He fell and died instantly. Given the state in which the plane was left, it was impossible to know what problems had caused the pilot to decide to parachute. As for the breakage of the parachute, it was indicated that it must have been opened too early by the pilot, tearing due to the strong reaction of the deployment.

On 6 May, the same types of services continued. At Seschtschinkaja, at 06:00, several Il-2s strafed the airfield, and, shortly afterwards, it was Pe-2s that, flying at about 3,000m, bombed it in three passes. Then, at 10:00, taking advantage of a period of calm, Lieutenant Juan Roselló was honoured and buried in the airfield's war cemetery. But, at 16:00, a large formation of Soviet aircraft (20 Il-2s, six LaGG-3s, 14 LaGG-5s and 45 Pe-2s) was spotted by the *Freya* heading for the Seschtschinskaja base. It was the largest formation of Soviet aircraft ever seen. On its entry, the Il-2 that started at low altitude was hit by the flak, which was cut in two with an accurate shot from the 88mm, followed by a Pe-2 and another Il-2, also hit by the flak.

Shortly before the alarm was raised, Captain José Ramón Gavilán Ponce de León and Ensign Alfonso Teixidor had taken off for a free fighter mission. Captain Gavilán recounted years later:

> We had taken off on an alarm and free fighter mission, as we had to be constantly in the air to repel Soviet attacks. When we were in the vicinity of Kirov, we received the order to return to the field and intercept some planes that were attacking it. I spotted them almost vertically and dived for a Pe-2, which seemed to be flying some way behind the others. I began shooting at it on the first pass, but without much correction, seeing that I was hitting it with my shots, but without causing any serious damage. I manoeuvred quickly and managed to catch its tail again; I approached to a distance of about sixty metres and saw that it was falling to the ground, noticeably

10 Arráez Cerdá, 'Les Espagnols de la Luftwaffe', 18, p.69.

Lieutenant José Ramón Gavilán of the 3rd Blue Squadron has just taken over one of the Bf 109 F-2 *Zacutos* from the 2nd Squadron, which handed over 10 in airworthy condition and four under repair. In the background are the German Fw 190s that shared the airfield with the Spaniards.

> touched, although I could not confirm the grid in which it fell. I was lucky, because I did not blind myself from seeing where it landed, and figured that the game must be close by. I turned my neck and sure enough, a protective LaGG-3 was trying to take advantage of its better position; I performed a combat turn and managed to get close to it. The pilot must have been pretty inexperienced, because it did not take me long to shoot him down. I called my partner, Ensign Teixidor, to meet me, but he said he could not because he was in combat.[11]

But what the captain could not imagine was that *El Retaco* was surely saving his life. According to Teixidor's memories:

> When Gavilán shot down the LaGG-3, I saw that one had stuck to his tail, I gassed up and went whaling on it. The Russian noticed, pulled into the sun to dazzle me, and then reversed to get into a good position. But I caught his tail again; you could tell that the man was no novice, as he did not give me any good angle for a shot, since when I was going to get it, he made a half-barrel. On the third shot I swore he would not get away from me: I anticipated his defensive manoeuvre, fired with everything I had and hit him; I do not remember where, but I hit him. He fell in our area, was captured alive and taken to our base. His name was Mikhail Koropkovo, 22 years old, a well-built guy. I think his biggest disappointment was not that I shot him down but that he had not shot down Gavilán like he thought. He was decorated with the Order of the Red Banner.[12]

Two more victories occurred that day, one by Lieutenant Azqueta, who set off in pursuit of five Il-2s returning to their base after bombing. He managed to catch up with them near Vitebsk, attacking the one on the right of the formation and making three passes at it: the first one a little higher by the tail and the other two also by the tail but lower than the Russian. In the last one, he observed how pieces of the Il-2 detached and how it started to emit black smoke and rapidly lose altitude. Just then, Azqueta was attacked by two LaGG-5s, and he evaded in a quick turn, seeing at that moment how the Il-2 crashed to the ground.

11 Arráez Cerdá, 'Les Espagnols de la Luftwaffe', 18, pp.69–70.
12 Arráez Cerdá, 'Les Espagnols de la Luftwaffe', 18, p.70.

The hunter and his prey. Ensign Alfonso Teixidor (right) talks with Captain Mikhail Koropkovo (centre), thanks to the German interpreter (who has a cigarette in his hand), after having shot down his LaGG-3.

Arrest of Mikhail Koropkovo, the Soviet pilot decorated with the Order of the Red Flag and shot down by Ensign Alfonso Teixidor '*El Retaco*' on 6 May 1943.

The two best pilots of the 3rd Blue Squadron, Captain Hevia and Lieutenant Azqueta, with one of the new Fw 190s that had been delivered to them.

The other victory was achieved by Lieutenant Alejandro Pérez González, who also attacked the Il-2s returning to their lines. He did so by positioning himself behind the tail of the one on the right of the group and somewhat behind the rest. Two hundred metres away, he shot it down, although one of its crew managed to parachute out.

On 7 May, the Seschtschinkaja airfield received warning of enemy aircraft, and the alarm pair, formed by Captain Antonio Alós Herrero and Lieutenant Luis Azqueta Brunet, took off. Once in the air, they received a warning that the enemy planes were about 10km north-west of the camp. They went after them and attacked them repeatedly. Reaching the vertical of the airfield, they had to get out of there, as the flak was firing at full intensity without distinguishing between friend and foe. They then resumed their attack, and Captain Alós shot at two Il-2s that had separated from their formation, hitting one of them on his third pass, which crashed. For his part, Lieutenant Azqueta, amidst explosions from the flak, attacked one at the precise moment that it dropped its bombs on the field and clearly observed how his shells hit the Il-2, knocking it down.

The days of 8–10 May were spent with the usual alarm services and free fighters, which passed without any major incident.

On 11 May, *Staffel* 26 of JG 54 took over Smolensk from the Spanish aircraft, which returned to Seschtschinkaja, where at last the entire 3rd Squadron was complete.

With the offensive unleashed by the Soviets, the protection of the He 111s and Ju 88s virtually ended, and an endless series of free fighter and alarm services began. The Russians, who had begun with heavy and continuous night bombing raids on the base, switched over the next few days to daylight bombing, some of them very heavy indeed. These attacks were of two types. In one of them, they did so at low altitude, taking advantage of the opportunity to reach the airfield undetected, and used Il-2s protected by LaGG-3s and LaGG-5s. They calculated their arrival at dawn both to make it difficult for the flak to fire and to ensure that few fighters would take off to repel their attack, and this was the case, as on most occasions only the alarm pair could do so. The fighters arrived earlier and kept flying over the field at altitudes between 100–500m, trying to avoid as much as possible the alarm aircraft's take-off by strafing them. The bombers soon followed and attacked at low altitude, using 100kg bombs and strafing.

Once the Il-2 attack was over, the fighters continued over the vertical of the field to prevent the German and Spanish planes from reaching them before they reached their lines. The 3rd Squadron, in these attacks, nevertheless managed to take off and fight quite successfully.

The second type of attack was very different and did not seek surprise but air superiority, using a large number of aircraft. It used to start at 19:00, the enemy entering the field with the sun on their tail. They first attacked with a

At the Orel airfield, Lieutenant Luis Azqueta poses next to the Bf 109 F with Werk N.6742, camouflaged for the winter season.

formation of Il-2s in low-flying flight while a large number of fighters flew at 500–5,000m. The Il-2s made a single pass and returned to their lines, always protected by their fighters. Then, at 1,500–2,000m, large formations of Pe-2s appeared and bombed, again with heavy fighter protection, generally making two passes. Once the bombing was over, after 10 or 15 minutes, a fast reconnaissance plane would appear to photograph the field and check the results obtained.

The rest of May was spent between alarm and free fighter services, although it was mostly the former ones since Russian bombers visited the field daily. Granted, sometimes when they met the Fw 190s in the air, they passed them by and moved on to other targets.

June would be the month with the greatest number of victories for the 3rd Squadron, a total of 22, although with the loss of Lieutenant Alejandro Pérez González.

1 June began with a sultry heat that had begun to replace the terrible cold. A few alarm services were carried out without incident, and only a formation of DB-3s was seen to the north of the airfield looking for other targets. The following day, the alarm services were repeated. In one of them, Captain Hevia and Ensign Teixidor saw some Il-2s flying with fighter escort in the distance and decided to go after them. They flew as fast as possible and, 20 minutes later, managed to catch up with them. However, when they were about to attack them, the Spaniards were intercepted by a large number of enemy fighters. Given the distance from their base, Hevia and Teixidor abandoned the attack.

On 3 June, an American-made Douglas Boston reconnaissance plane passed over the field, the first time such a plane had ever been seen. At night, before the alarm sirens sounded, 18 DB-3s and one SB-2, using flares, began dropping bombs on the airfield.

On 4 June, there were no alarms, and the day passed peacefully. However, at dawn the next day, a large number of He 111 and Ju 88 bombers began concentrating on the field. They were to leave at night to bomb the factories, arms depots and military installations in the town of Gorky.

6 June dawned with sultry heat and the threat of a thunderstorm, but this did not prevent the same services from continuing. In a free fighter, Ensign Javier Mª Guibert sighted two LaGG-3s and managed to get behind one, which he shot down after two passes. Then, at 19:00, a twin-engine Boston reconnaissance aircraft made a low-flying pass over the field and, shortly afterwards, the pilot trusting to his luck, repeated it. However, in this second case, it was shot down by the flak. The Spaniards curiously approached it and could see the American emblems covered by the red star of the USSR.

On 7 June, news was received that the 1st Patrol of the 4th Squadron had just arrived in Berlin. Despite the joy of knowing that they would soon return to Spain, the 3rd Squadron's guard was not lowered at all. On 8 June, at 01:00,

50 planes carried out an attack in which they dropped more than 300 explosive and incendiary bombs, which destroyed one of the squadron's Fw 190 A-2s, although the German losses were greater. The same day, at 19:00, an Il-2 formation and another of Pe-2s appeared with a large fighter protection, a total of 56 aircraft, unloading some 400 bombs that, fortunately, did not cause any damage to the 3rd Squadron. Given the virulence of the attack, the order was given that all available aircraft should be ready to take off immediately. In the meantime, already in the air was the alarm pair, formed by Captain Hevia and Lieutenant Julio Pérez Muñoz, who immediately went into combat. Captain Hevia managed to get behind a LaGG-3 and easily shot it down with his second burst. He then went for another, but this combat was very different, as he faced the best pilot he could find in Russia. According to his memories:

When the Fw 190s began to be delivered to the 3rd Squadron, Lieutenant Julio Pérez Muñoz did not hesitate to climb on top of one of them to take this photograph.

> Taking advantage of the inertia of the first fight, I gained altitude easily; when I was at about 7,000 metres, I saw a LaGG-3 or a MiG-5. That guy knew what he was doing. He was not the kind of guy we were used to encountering. It was a real dogfight, as soon as we were at 7,000 metres, and then up again. Two or three times my plane turned to the right, because I was going too high. That man, and this I think was what lost him, would shoot from any position. Several times I saw him shoot at me in inverted flight. At more than one moment I thought that, in one of those, he would be accompanied by luck … and goodbye. However, it was with me because, except for the first few moments when I shot down the LaGG-3, my ammunition was almost intact. Your luck will run out, I thought when I could. And it did run out. At that point he veered into his area and started to climb. I had a hard time catching him, but I was willing to do it, even if I ran out of fuel, and I had to make it before he got into a cloud layer in front of us where, if I did, I would have lost him. I had him in range, but I wanted to get closer. Three seconds before he entered the clouds I shot at him. It was a continuous burst with everything I had, four guns and two machine guns. I was sure that I had hit him.
>
> When I returned to the field, I explained what had happened, but I dared not take it for granted, as I had not seen him crash. I had almost given up hope of writing it down when, late in the afternoon, our interpreter Hombach reported that he had received a call that a Russian fighter had crashed nearby. From the time and place, there was no doubt: it was mine.[13]

With these two victories, Captain Hevia had scored 10 shootdowns, making him the squadron's top ace.

His wingman, Lieutenant Pérez Muñoz, went after the Il-2s, but, when he saw his protection fighter above them, he climbed up and managed to get behind one of the LaGG-5s. He shot it down with an accurate long burst, not cutting it off until he saw how the Russian began a vertical dive from which he did not come out and crashed to the ground.

13 Arráez Cerdá, 'Les Espagnols de la Luftwaffe', 18, pp.71–72.

Captain Hevia of the 3rd Blue Squadron poses next to the tail of his Bf 109 F. Five victory bars are shown for the Spanish pilot, who would eventually achieve 12 victories, the highest number of victories achieved by Spanish pilots in the skies of the USSR. (Courtesy of Almena)

Lieutenant Rafael Calleja observed how one of the LaGG-5s tried to position itself behind the tail of Captain Hevia's plane, so he quickly manoeuvred and positioned himself behind it, firing two bursts that shot it down. He then headed for one of the Pe-2s, which he easily shot down, before returning home due to engine failure. Another pilot also managed a double. It was Captain Gavilán, who first went for a straggling LaGG-3 and easily shot it down with his first few shots. He climbed again and then spotted the Il-2s trying to escape back to their lines, so he attacked one. After three passes, it crash-landed violently next to a German flak battery.

In the same combat, Lieutenant Bernardo Meneses opted for the Pe-2s and attacked one of the last of the formation, which he managed to set on fire and shoot down after several passes. For his part, Lieutenant Azqueta saw an Il-2 leaving the field after strafing it and went after it, subsequently shooting it down. He was then attacked by a group of LaGG-3s but eventually, and not without difficulty, managed to get away from them. Finally, Lieutenant Alejandro Pérez González also noticed that a Pe-2 was lagging behind and took the opportunity to collimate and shoot it with everything he had, setting it on fire immediately. Given its vulnerability, it fell to the ground. However, a LaGG-3 had managed to get close to him and shoot at him from a good angle, so his white Fw 190 A-2 No.3 caught fire. Parachuting down, his uncontrolled plane hit him with its rudder and gave him a severe shock from which he was unable to get out, and he died.

On this day, they had achieved 10 shootdowns with only one loss, and so the 3rd Squadron had surpassed 50 victories.

On 9 June, at 15:00, Lieutenant Alejandro Pérez González received posthumous honours and was buried in the base's war cemetery. The rest of the day passed without further incident.

Captain Gavilán (white coat) listens to his mechanics' report moments before boarding his aircraft (a Bf 109 F) for a combat mission. The first Fw 190s delivered to the 3rd Squadron can be seen in the background.

Lieutenant Alejandro Pérez González of the 3rd Squadron was killed in action on 8 June 1943. The brave Spanish pilot's Fw 190 A-2 ('3' white) was shot down by a LaGG-3, the pilot being hit by his own plane while parachuting.

At 07:00 on 10 June, a Pe-2 made a photographic reconnaissance at an altitude of 5,400m so as not to be intercepted. This likely meant that the day was going to be quite busy, and it was, as the Russians carried out the biggest attack to date. At 19:00, the warning was received that Russian planes were approaching, and the Fw 190s began to take off. At the same moment, the first Soviet planes began strafing the field while the flak was firing, which in a few moments managed to shoot down four of them. A total of 68 Soviet aircraft attacked both the Blue Squadron's Fw 190s and the *Luftwaffe* aircraft sharing the airfield, but the fighters were already in the air, and the fighting began immediately.

Lieutenant Guibert, who was Lieutenant Pérez Muñoz's wingman, launched himself against one of the LaGG-3s, firing at it and hitting it squarely. It then fell in the vicinity of the field, and Guibert achieved his first victory.

Ensign Aldecoa was the last to take off, as he recounted:

> I took off last, as my aircraft was in the hangar, the situation was a bit unpleasant, because I had to go alone and, on top of that, there was an enemy fighter that, if it spotted me taking off, would surely shoot me down. Once I got up to altitude, I saw two LaGG-5s coming through the clouds; I returned to the field and joined two Fw 190s that were diving towards some Il-2s. Just ahead of them I saw two LaGG-3s that were a

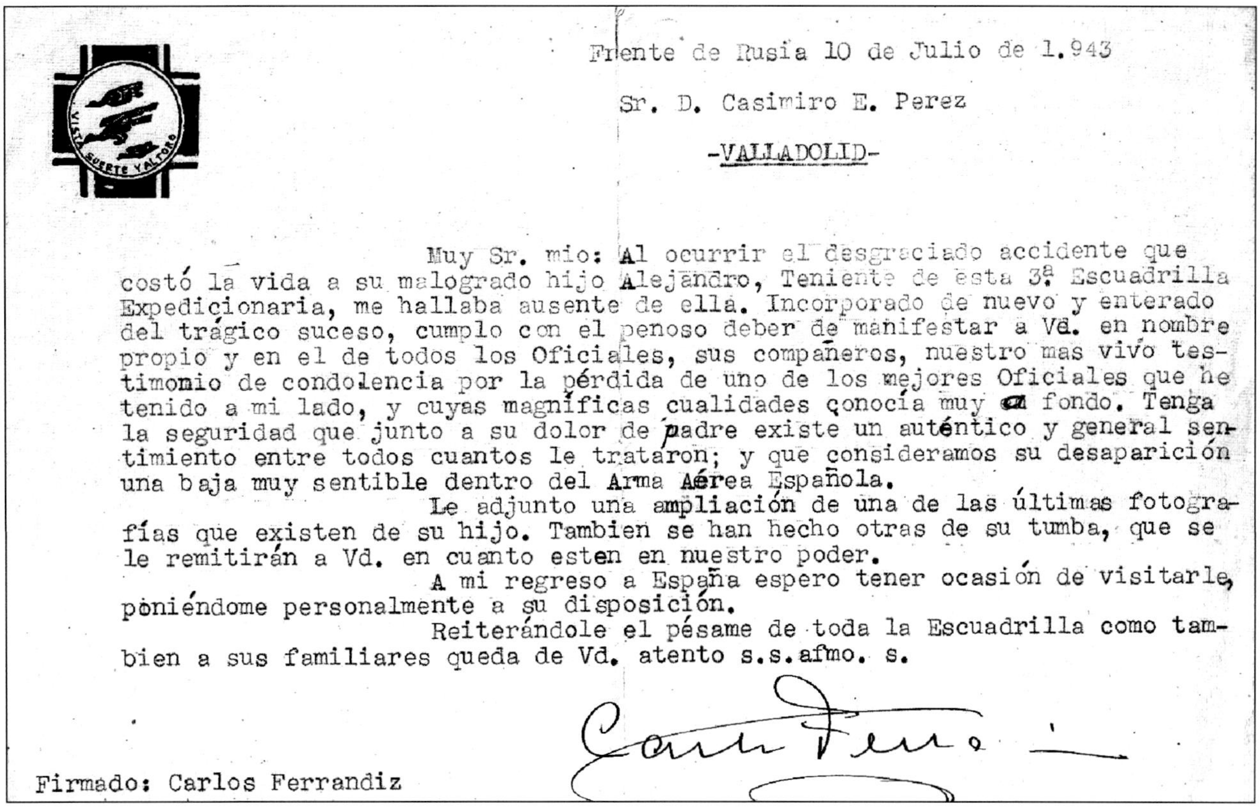

Frente de Rusia 10 de Julio de 1.943

Sr. D. Casimiro E. Perez

-VALLADOLID-

Muy Sr. mio: Al ocurrir el desgraciado accidente que costó la vida a su malogrado hijo Alejandro, Teniente de esta 3ª Escuadrilla Expedicionaria, me hallaba ausente de ella. Incorporado de nuevo y enterado del trágico suceso, cumplo con el penoso deber de manifestar a Vd. en nombre propio y en el de todos los Oficiales, sus compañeros, nuestro mas vivo testimonio de condolencia por la pérdida de uno de los mejores Oficiales que he tenido a mi lado, y cuyas magníficas cualidades conocía muy a fondo. Tenga la seguridad que junto a su dolor de padre existe un auténtico y general sentimiento entre todos cuantos le trataron; y que consideramos su desaparición una baja muy sentible dentro del Arma Aérea Española.

Le adjunto una ampliación de una de las últimas fotografías que existen de su hijo. Tambien se han hecho otras de su tumba, que se le remitirán a Vd. en cuanto esten en nuestro poder.

A mi regreso a España espero tener ocasión de visitarle, poniéndome personalmente a su disposición.

Reiterándole el pésame de toda la Escuadrilla como tambien a sus familiares queda de Vd. atento s.s.afmo. s.

Firmado: Carlos Ferrandiz

Letter from the 3rd Squadron documenting the shooting down and death of Lieutenant Alejandro Pérez González, addressed to the pilot's family.

> little lower. I fired at one of them with cannons and machine guns; I saw how the engine irons began jumping and it fell into a sharp ring. I also watched Lieutenant Meneses shoot down another one and when I was distracted watching the spectacle, I felt hits on my plane; they were Il-2s that had fallen behind. One hit me in the fuel tank, two in the fuselage and a 20 mm cannon shot hit the rudder, forcing me to return to the field.[14]

Lieutenant Meneses had indeed shot down another LaGG-3, but this would not be his only victory. He also went after the Il-2s that were returning to their lines and flying at about 200m, attacking the last of the group, which he damaged until it crashed to the ground moments later.

Captain Gavilán attacked an Il-2 patrol that was about to strafe the field. He fired at the last of the formation, which tried to escape, but Gavilán followed up with his guns, sending it into a tailspin and crash.

Captain Hevia went for the Pe-2s, and, once well behind the tail of one, he fired at it with all his weapons and immediately shot it down. He then went to the nearest LaGG-3s and attacked the one on the right of the group, shooting it down.

Ensign Aldecoa tells a comrade from the 3rd Squadron how he managed a shootdown. Between his time with the 3rd and 4th Squadrons, this pilot shot down a total of seven enemy aircraft.

14 Arráez Cerdá, 'Les Espagnols de la Luftwaffe', 18, p.73.

Generaloberst Ritter von Greim's visit to the 3rd Blue Squadron. The photo shows several of the squadron's pilots, from left to right: Captain Alós, Captain Ozores, Captain Gavilán, Major Ferrándiz, *Generaloberst* Ritter von Greim, Lieutenant Calleja, Lieutenant Pérez, Ensign Teixidor, Lieutenant Meneses and Captain Hevia.

Vara de Rey, recently promoted to lieutenant, attacked the LaGG-3s. Since his cannons were not working, he only used his machine guns and hit one of them head-on, which crashed after a steep dive.

For his part, Lieutenant Azqueta noticed that a LaGG-3 had positioned itself behind the tail of a Fw 190 and quickly headed towards it, attacking it and managing to shoot it down.

Finally, Captain Alós attacked a pair of LaGG-3s, shooting the one on the right and knocking it down.

Ten new victories had been achieved without a single casualty. The mechanics, who had seen the spectacle since it had taken place over the same airfield, rushed towards the landing planes. The pilots were exhausted but happy and satisfied.

They had barely finished commenting on the incidents suffered when, at 21:00, only two hours after the start of the previous attack, the camp was again attacked, this time by 72 DB-3 and DB-7 aircraft that, flying at 1,600–4,500m, dropped 900 explosive bombs, 80 incendiary bombs and 13 lighting bombs. There were numerous fires and many casualties, although none among the Spanish. This time, there was little that the exhausted Spanish and German pilots could do, and the base suffered considerable damage. Only one aircraft was shot down, done by a *Luftwaffe* night fighter.

Early the next morning, a Pe-2 appeared at 6,000m to photograph the airfield and check the damage. The photos must not have turned out very well, as it flew over the airfield again at 16:00, although this time shot down by a German fighter. 12–13 June passed quietly, but, in the evenings, the bombing was repeated, although with less intensity than in the previous days. In the bombing raid of the latter evening, two of the Spanish Fw 190s were disabled. On 14 June, not a single Soviet plane appeared.

On 15 June, the first pilots of the 4th Squadron finally arrived in the new Ju 52 liaison plane: Captain Felice Galarza Sánchez, Lieutenants Fernando Sánchez-Arjona Courtoy, Gerardo Escalante de la Lastra and Francisco Valiente Zárraga and Ensign José Mateos Recio.

The next two days, the Russians carried out their usual night attacks, but the flak and night fighters shot down two of them. On 18 June, a free fighter and orientation service was conducted for the 4th Squadron pilots, which was repeated the following day. However, during the night of 19 June, the Soviets destroyed one of the Fw 190s and damaged two others on the ground. From 20 to 23 June, there were no night bombing raids, and the services that were carried out, without incident, were free fighter and guidance services for the pilots of the 4th Squadron. On 24 June, bombers were protected in the Spatember area, and, at night, the Russians sent reconnaissance planes over the field, but German night fighters were on the lookout and shot down two.

On 25 June, a farewell party was held for the first echelon of the 3rd Squadron that would return to Spain, receiving from the German command the decorations that they had deserved.

On 5 July, the 3rd Squadron completed its activities in Russia. The 4th Squadron officially took over representing the Spanish EdA on the Eastern Front, with its base initially at the Seschtschinskaja airfield. Although, the day before that, Lieutenant Meneses had fought against two LaGG-5s, shooting down one of them.

According to Hans Werner Neulen, at the official farewell of the 3rd Blue Squadron, JG 51 *Kommodore* Karl-Gottfried Nordmann gave this heartfelt speech to the Spaniards:

> Apart from the hardships of war, by your steely will you have overcome the extreme winter cold to which you are not accustomed, the dirt and mud of spring, and the dust and heat of summer. You have done your duty as only soldiers know how, and the proof and reward of this conduct has been the magnificent success of the squadron ...[15]

The 3rd Squadron's days in Russia were over, although some of its pilots would remain there for some time attached to the 4th Squadron. They were Lieutenants Vicente Aldecoa Lecanda, Javier Mª Guibert Amor, Bernardo Meneses Ozores and Ruy Ozores Ochoa '*El Barón*'.

The 3rd Squadron participated in 1,716 flight missions, flying 112 combat sorties and shooting down 62 aircraft. Its number of shootdowns was considerably higher than those of the two previous squadrons due to the increased number of Soviet aircraft in the area where the Spanish were located. On the negative side, the squadron lost five pilots.

Ensign Guibert stroking one of the small Russian horses used for a variety of tasks at the airfield where the Spaniards were based.

15 Hans Werner Neulen, *In the Skies of Europe: Air Forces Allied to the Luftwaffe 1939–1945* (Ramsbury: The Crowood Press, 2000), p.282.

4

4th Squadron

The 4th Blue Squadron was created on 1 April 1943 at Alcalá de Henares, Madrid, the airfield there designated for their concentration and training. In command was Major Mariano Cuadra Medina, who was a veteran of the GCE (although he had not achieved any aerial victories). As inspector commander, he immediately began to appoint the pilots who would make up the squadron. They were Captain Felipe Galarza Sánchez, who was the squadron commander, Lieutenants Gerardo Escalante de la Lastra, Francisco Valiente Zárraga and Lorenzo Lucas Fernández-Peña and Ensign José Mateos Recio. The rest of the pilots would join the squadron a few days later. In Alcalá de Henares, they completed a month of training with the help of veteran personnel from previous squadrons using CR.32 biplanes and Bf 109 E monoplanes (in free fighter, combat, photographic and live firing practice). After 306 training flights, they were considered ready to leave by train for the Colomiers air base, where some of the pilots of the 1st Patrol of the 4th Squadron arrived in mid-May. The choice of the Colomiers air base rather than St-Jean-d'Angély was due to the fact that the latter did not have Fw 190s but only Bf 109s. At the Colomiers airfield (on the outskirts of Toulouse and the former site of the Dewoitine aircraft factory, where the Germans had their so-called 'Fighter Reserve Group and Night Fighter School'), they spent a month completing their training period under the guidance of the *Luftwaffe*'s expert pilot *Hauptmann* Walter Stengel of JG 51.

The orders were to reduce training as much as possible, as the needs of the front were urgent and, moreover, Major Ferrándiz had recommended it because of his experience with the 3rd Squadron. In addition, the 3rd Squadron sent Lieutenant Ramón Luca de Tena to teach them the 'tricks' that this front required.

The Oath of Allegiance to the *Führer* for the Eastern Campaign took place on 16 May and was presided over by the German ace Hermann Graf. The in-flight training period with the Fw 190 was approximately seven hours per pilot, after which the Spaniards of the 1st Patrol were considered fit to replace their comrades of the 3rd Squadron. Therefore, on 6 June, they left for the front in a Ju 52 registered 'CJ+AC' and piloted by Fernando Arrechea Belfunce and Agustín Ortiz, arriving on 15 June at their destination at Seschtschinskaja after a stopover in Berlin.

On 15 June, after 228 flights, the staff and 2nd Patrol of the 4th Blue Squadron finished their training in Alcalá de Henares. Without further delay, and after preparing the men for the journey, on 17 June, they left by train for Toulouse under the command of Major Cuadra. The pilots were Captain José Llaca Álvarez, Lieutenants Manuel Sánchez-Tabernero, Diego Vigueras Murube, Dámaso Arango López and Pedro Lacalle Orellana and Ensign Eduardo García Amigó. After transferring to the

The leader of the 4th Blue Squadron, Major Mariano Cuadra, was the second Spanish ace of the five squadrons, with 10 enemy aircraft shot down.

Major Mariano Cuadra Medina conversing in the vicinity of a Ju 52. Note the coat of arms with the colours of the Spanish flag, carried by the members of the Blue Squadron (and the Blue Division), on his right arm.

Act of the Oath of Allegiance to the *Führer* for the Russian campaign by members of the 4th Blue Squadron, held at the Toulouse–Colomiers airfield and presided over by the German ace Hermann Graf, seen on the right in a steel helmet.

After the oath of allegiance, Spanish officers of the 4th Blue Squadron chat with German officers as they pass in front of a pair of Focke Wulf Fw 190s, with which they have trained there.

Colomiers air base, on 18 June, they began their training period, which was quite brief since, on 4 July, they arrived in the Spanish Ju 52 (along with the military chaplain Captain Gonzalo de los Ríos and Troop Lieutenant Julio Perez Caballero) at the Seschtschinskaja air base.

The aircraft used by the Spanish were the Fw 190 A-2 and A-3, while the Germans were already using more modern models such as the Fw 190 A-4 and A-5.

As with the previous squadrons, it was very useful for the new pilots arriving at the front to share combat missions with pilots from the prior squadron in order to improve their learning. Therefore, four pilots from the previous squadron (Aldecoa, Meneses, Guibert and Ozores) remained attached until the arrival of the last patrol of the 4th Blue Squadron. The combat experience in Russia of the attached 3rd Blue Squadron pilots was demonstrated by the 10 air victories they achieved between July and August. For example, Aldecoa added to his one aircraft shot down with the 3rd Squadron six more aircraft while attached to the 4th Squadron.

The logistical aspect of the Blue Squadron was also improved, so a new Ju 52 joined the existing one to replace the previous one during technical inspections and to better coordinate the Madrid–Berlin flights.

The 4th Squadron joined the front at a crucial moment of the war on the Eastern Front, on 5 July 1943, right at the start of Operation Citadel (*Zitadelle*) with the German summer offensive on Kursk (at 04:40, the German artillery unleashed a

Captain José Llaca with the Fw 190 A-2 with which he will take off for one of his regular war services.

The Spanish mechanics work hard to get the white Fw 190 A-2 No.21 ready for service. Some details of its engine can be seen.

The white Fw 190 No.5 of the 4th Blue Squadron during a mission. None of the aircraft of the 4th Squadron carried any Spanish emblem to distinguish it from the other German *Luftwaffe* aircraft.

Mechanics of the 4th Squadron working on the engine of one of their Fw 190 A-2s.

very intense cannonade on the Soviet positions, a prelude to their infantry attack). Like the 2nd and 3rd Squadrons, the 4th Squadron was incorporated by JG 51 into *VIII. Fliegerkorps*. The *Luftwaffe* had five squadrons in the sector of the front where the Spanish were: the Blue Squadron, I./JG 54, I./JG 51, II./JG 51 and III./JG 51 – a total of about 140 Fw 190s (of which only 88 were in service).

The 4th Blue Squadron had Commander Cuadra and 19 pilots, and its ground echelon had four officers, 12 NCOs and 116 soldiers. The total number of men was 152, making it the largest squadron that Spain sent to Russia. The 4th Squadron was distributed as follows:

Staff: Commander-in-Chief Major Cuadra
1st Patrol: Captain Galarza, Lieutenants Lucas, Valiente, Sánchez-Arjona and Escalante and Ensign Mateos
2nd Patrol: Captain Llaca, Lieutenants Sánchez, Lacalle, Vigueras and Arango and Ensigns García and Chicharro
3rd Patrol: Captain Borrás, Lieutenants Serra, Cavanilles and Pareja and Ensigns Estébanez and Recasens.

Of the pilots, only one had achieved aerial victories in the GCE, Lieutenant Serra, with four aircraft shot down. Some other pilots had participated in air combat during the GCE: Captain Llaca and Lieutenants Vigueras, Lacalle and Arango.

The Spanish squadron was ordered to be ready for a general alarm as soon as it joined the front line. The Spaniards began flying their Fw 190s on 5 July, although only Major Cuadra sighted two enemy aircraft but without shooting them down.

The following day (6 July) dawned splendidly, and the services began to follow one after the other. Lieutenant Lorenzo Lucas Fernández-Peña (No.20) and his wingman, Lieutenant Pedro '*Perico*' Lacalle Orellana (No.14), took off for a free fighter service. A short time later, Lieutenant Lucas observed how his wingman's plane was leaving a trail of smoke and ordered him by radio to return to the field, but, when '*Perico*' Lacalle was about to obey, his plane's engine stopped dead in its tracks. He was flying at about 1,000m, so he glided to land on the terrain he thought best, but the touchdown was very abrupt. Fw 190 No.14 was badly damaged, and its pilot received severe neck injuries that made it impossible for him to fly again, so he was evacuated to Spain. In the Spas-Demensk sector, Captain Gavilán was flying with Lieutenant Manuel Sánchez-Tabernero, who was leaving on his first war service, his mission being that of a free fighter. When the commander gave the warning that enemy planes were coming towards them, he started the attack at full speed, and his point tried to follow him, but he fell behind. When the lieutenant thought he saw the Russian planes, Sánchez-Tabernero realised that they were behind him and lower down; he tried to get them off him, turning with the engine at full throttle, but there was no way. Just as he thought that

Upon arrival at the Russian airfield at Seschtschinskaja, the members of the 4th Squadron are reviewed by the German command.

Lieutenant Lorenzo Lucas Fernández-Peña of the 4th Squadron in the cockpit of his aircraft, ready for take-off. This brave pilot managed to shoot down six enemy aircraft.

they were going to shoot him down, Sánchez-Tabernero realised that they were actually Fw 190s and to top it all off … Spaniards! Since he had lost altitude, he climbed up with the idea of finding Gavilán, calling him on the radio. When he got no reply, he set course for the field, but, after a few minutes, the red light for low fuel came on. Recognising the terrain over which he was flying, he launched the canopy and landed with the landing gear inside without any major problems. He was picked up the next day by a Fieseler Fi 156 *Storch* piloted by Captain José Llaca.

On 6 July, the 3rd Squadron began its return to Spain, although Lieutenants Ruy Ozores Ochoa '*El Barón*', Vicente Aldecoa Lecanda, Javier Mª Guibert Aznar and Bernardo Meneses Orozco remained attached to the 4th Squadron.

Lieutenants Lorenzo Lucas and Manuel Sánchez-Tabernero of the 4th Squadron. Both pilots managed to shoot down six enemy aircraft each.

On 7 July, the 4th Squadron would achieve its first shootdown, by Ensign José Mateos Recio. According to how he remembered it:

Ensign José Mateos Recio was the pilot of the first shootdown carried out by the 4th Squadron, a LaGG-5 on 7 July 1943. He also shot down three more: a LaGG-5, a LaGG-3 and an Il-2.

> We took off at about 18:00 to protect a Fw 189. We were told it was on a photographic reconnaissance mission over several Soviet camps. Suddenly we noticed that it was dropping several bombs and diving at full speed. We lost sight of it. Lucas rose to my left towards the sun and we saw seven or eight fighters, which looked like LaGG-5s. They had seen him, but not me, because of the sun. This was my chance. The last one passed in front of me, I got on its tail and fired at it with cannon and machine guns, so that it exploded so close to me that I got oil all over the cockpit glass. As I turned left to find Lucas, I saw a parachute and, as I was very nervous about the events, I asked Lucas if it was him. How was he going to answer me? An interminable few seconds passed, until I heard: 'that is the plane you shot down, I am going to your right and higher'. I saw him at once and came closer; we made a sharp turn and went into the clouds, throwing off the rest of the fighters that were chasing us. When we reached the field, I made a pass and, after landing, they carried me out on their shoulders, like bullfighters …[1]

With Operation Citadel already underway, the Spanish were immersed in an area of the front with a high level of air activity, as could be confirmed by the high number of victories they would achieve against the Soviets. Despite the Spaniards' desire to be in continuous action, due to their 'inexperienced' condition at the front, the Spanish pilots were assigned to bases relatively far from the Kursk salient. A patrol with five pilots (Captain Ruy Ozores and Lieutenants Francisco Valiente and Dámaso Arango, Ensign José Mateos and veteran of the 3rd Squadron Lieutenant Bernardo Meneses) would be deployed in Bryansk, the closest to the Kursk salient from where they would operate between 12–21 July. Later, another patrol would be sent to Vitebsk, and the 3rd Patrol to its base in Seschtschinskaja. Due to the *Luftwaffe*'s continuing need for missions, orders were received that free fighters were to be flown by only two aircraft at a time in order to carry out as many missions as possible. At least two missions per day of one-and-a-half hours' duration were to be flown by the various pilots. The days had many daylight hours, so missions could start at 05:00 and finish at 23:00, to which must be added the Soviet night attacks on the German bases. Naturally, exhaustion would soon appear not only in the Spanish pilots but also in their *Luftwaffe* comrades.

On 13 July, two new victories were achieved. Lieutenant Manuel Sánchez-Tabernero recounted the first:

> We took off in two pairs on a free fighter mission; the first was made up of Major Mariano Cuadra and Ensign Eduardo García Amigó; I was with Ensign Aldecoa, one of the veterans of the Third. A short time into the flight, we spotted four LaGG-5s flying in formation at low altitude, about four hundred metres above the ground, because the cloud ceiling was quite low. We set a course towards them and what I have never seen before in my time at the front happened to us: three of the planes turned 180 degrees and the fourth continued towards us. As I watched, I was overjoyed to see the outcome of my first battle, inaugurating my personal locker; we crossed nose to nose and, before the first turn was over, I was on its tail. I was sure I would finish it off. I started firing at him with the machine guns and the two cannons; my tracers told me I was gaining on it and I thought that, at any moment, that plane would take a hit that would knock it to the ground. We continued to turn, and I found myself in a comfortable position on its tail, with the security of Aldecoa's protection, whom I could always see at my side. I was more and more sure that I would bring it down, because I was really playing with it: I would get as close as I wanted and, thinking it would be easier, I would put my nose in front of it and shoot. I let it move forwards and get into the beam of my machine guns, confident that I was frying it, but that big bird seemed armoured, or I missed some vital spot. I fired, according to what I was told when I reloaded the

1 Juan Arráez Cerdá, 'Les Espagnols de la Luftwaffe: Les Escadrilles Bleues', *Ciel de Guerre*, 19 (2011), p.8.

The white Fw 190 No.14 of Lieutenant Lacalle Orellana in the Seschtschinskaja field during the Battle of Kursk.

> armament, more than seven hundred and fifty shells, and I could not get it; Aldecoa, probably bored of turning to protect me, decided to pass over me and fired a single burst that cut off the tip of the right plane, immediately going into a tailspin from which it did not make more than one turn. Unfortunately, he was unable to parachute out, as we were too low.
>
> For me it was an unforgettable fight, but I was pretty shattered and I still have not been able to figure out why I did not hit that plane to the ground ...[2]

In a new service at 17:40, Lieutenant Sánchez-Tabernero took off again with Ensign García Amigó as his partner while the pair formed by Major Cuadra and Lieutenant Lorenzo Lucas awaited them in the air. As the four of them flew in open formation, they spotted nine LaGG-3s and immediately engaged in combat. With the first bursts, Lieutenant Lucas shot down one of the LaGG-3s, but the others were not so lucky. Sánchez-Tabernero was hit, and his engine began to leak oil, covering his windscreen and leaving him almost without visibility, so when he reached the field, he landed on the right. Ensign García Amigó was short of fuel and had to land at a German airfield, where he refuelled and then left for his base.

The fighting was continuous, and *Luftwaffe* casualties were high. The Spanish pilots were exhausted, which led Commander Cuadra to say that, if they continued at this rate and if luck did not help, the squadron would be forced to withdraw due to a lack of pilots.

14 July was a tragic day for the 4th Squadron, as two of its pilots were shot down. At 16:55, two pairs took off on escort duty for a He 111, the first formed by Major Cuadra and Ensign Amigó and the second by Lieutenant Sánchez-Tabernero and Ensign Aldecoa. When they were already behind enemy lines, a group of Soviet aircraft made up of LaGG-3s and LaGG-5s appeared. Cuadra was lucky and managed to get behind a LaGG-3, which he shot at and hit while listening to the radio as his point man, Ensign Amigó, said something to him, which he did not quite understand, about the petrol. Since they were only a short distance from Shisdra, well inside enemy lines, Cuadra ordered him to return to base. Unfortunately, neither the ensign, who was reported missing, nor his Fw 190 A-2 Werk N.2286 were ever heard from again.

As for the other pair, when the enemy fighter appeared, Sánchez-Tabernero gave Aldecoa the order to attack and headed for a LaGG-5, which he shot at with everything he had. Without realising that he had another on his tail, Sánchez-Tabernero was shot at and hit in his tail, as well as his left wing and cockpit, although fortunately he was unharmed. He

2 Arráez Cerdá, 'Les Espagnols de la Luftwaffe', 19, p.8.

One of the Focke Wulf Fw 190 A-2s of the 4th Squadron during the Battle of Kursk.

Members of the 4th Blue Squadron form up to await the arrival of *Kommodore* Nordmann, head of JG 51, at the Seschtschinskaja field in the summer of 1943.

Four excellent pilots belonging to the 4th Squadron: Major Cuadra, Captain Llaca and Lieutenants Serra and Lucas. Between them, they managed to shoot down 21 enemy aircraft.

escaped as best he could and reached an altitude of 5,000m. Confirming that his engine was slowing down and losing revolutions, he headed back without hesitation and with the thought that luck would be with him, but this was not the case because, when he was flying over his own territory, he was surprised by another LaGG-5. Without thinking twice, Sánchez-Tabernero pulled down and launched the cockpit to land on flat ground, close to the village of Chatkowo. As soon as his Fw 190 stopped 'ploughing' the ground, he jumped out and ran, as the Russian machine-gunned him. Fortunately, he was able to duck into a hole, and, not seeing him, the LaGG-5 left. He then went to a nearby village he had seen and was lucky enough that it was garrisoned by the Germans, with whom he spent the night. The next day, Sánchez-Tabernero was evacuated in a casualty truck to another location from where he was able to contact the squadron.

On the same 14 July, the last echelon of the 4th Squadron left Spain for France. While the 4th Squadron was not complete, personnel from the 3rd Squadron were still attached to it.

But there was no time for rest, and so, the following day, there was a new combat against four Il-2s escorted by five LaGG-3s, in which Lieutenant Lorenzo Lucas was able to shoot down one of the LaGG-3s. On 16 July, it was Lieutenant Fernando Sánchez-Arjona's turn to shoot down a LaGG-5. In addition, his point, Lieutenant Lorenzo Lucas, managed to repeat his shootdown from the previous day, this time a LaGG-5.

On 20 July, the patrol sent to the Bryansk camp returned to Seschtschinskaja during the day, but the joy of being all together was short-lived. On 22 July, another patrol – formed by Captain José Llaca, Lieutenants Arjona and Escalante and Ensigns Guibert and Aldecoa, accompanied by a group of specialists – was sent to the Vitebsk camp, located farther north. The Seschtschinskaja field was also bombed in the morning, and the Spanish lost Fw 190 No.20, which was hit squarely, and two others were slightly damaged.

On 26 July, Captain Galarza managed to shoot down a Yak-9, and, on 30 July, it was Lieutenant Dámaso Arango's turn to shoot down a LaGG-5.

Also on 30 July, a special order was issued by the *Mölders* unit upon achieving 6,000 German aerial victories, in which a summary was made of what had been done since the beginning of the war, highlighting the performance in the USSR and emphasising the performance of the Blue Squadrons: 'For more than a year now our Spanish comrades have

A couple of men from the 4th Squadron pose next to one of the Spanish unit's Fw 190 A-3s in summer camouflage. The Spanish pilots were very pleased with the performance and firepower of the Focke Wulf aircraft.

been at our side, animated by a tireless will to fight, overcoming all the numerous difficulties presented in their path and have contributed to help JG 51, with all enthusiasm, achieving the successes of which we are so proud.'[3]

The month of July ended with 487 war missions and 50 engagements, in which 11 victories were achieved, with the loss of two pilots: one wounded and the other missing.

The activity was exhausting for the pilots but no less so for the specialists and the rest of the squadron's ground staff, who had to work many days of more than 20 hours to keep their aircraft operational and whose breaks were threatened by bombings and attacks by enemy aircraft.

August was to be the most successful month of all for the Blue Squadrons: 44 victories and 640 war services, but which cost the lives of two pilots and another seriously wounded.

It all began on 1 August. At 03:15, Commander Cuadra and Captain Galarza took off, followed by Lieutenant Arango and Ensign Mateos, to protect three groups of He 111 bombers that had to operate in the Seschtschinskaja sector. As expected, Russian fighters made their appearance, and, in the ensuing firefight, Cuadra shot down a LaGG-3. In the afternoon, the He 111 escort was repeated. The pilots were the same as in the morning, who were now joined by Lieutenant Sánchez-Tabernero, as he recalled:

> When we were protecting the bombers, we saw three LaGG-3s. I went into the last one with my team leader, Captain Galarza, and it did not take me long to get behind one of the fighters. I fired at it with machine guns and cannons. I saw that the tracers were hitting it and it immediately went into a tailspin, but very sharply. We were very high up and I tried not to lose sight of it as it went down. Because of the difference in speed, I could not get upwind of it and it left me behind: I had to make a wide turn that made me lose it momentarily; when I tried to catch up with it again, near the ground, I saw the explosion against the ground; I had no doubt that it was mine. When I landed, I was approached by Major Cuadra; he claimed that he had seen a LaGG-3 crash, but also observed a German fighter following close behind. I claimed that I had only fired one burst and it was not approved …[4]

If July had been an intense month of air combat, August began with even greater intensity. From 3 to 8 August, multiple air clashes with the Spanish increased the number of aircraft shot down by the Spaniards. It was necessary to always

3 Caballero and Guillén, *Escuadrillas azules en Rusia*, p.86.
4 Arráez Cerdá, 'Les Espagnols de la Luftwaffe', 19, p.13.

keep the Spanish planes in the air, so all the pilots of the squadron flew at least two missions a day, each lasting an hour and a quarter. The imperative need for air support of the *Wehrmacht* and *Waffen-SS* troops required, in some cases, that the German (and Spanish) fighters act in ground attack missions. Thus, during 3–8 August, 12 victories were achieved, and the pilots had to work hard to meet all the needs that arose, eventually having to operate from the Prost and Smolensk fields.

On 3 August, Ensign José Mateos shot down a LaGG-3, and Lieutenant Fernando Sánchez-Arjona (No.25) took part in a strafing service on the ground. The following day, Lieutenant Gerardo Escalante managed to shoot down a LaGG-5, and Lieutenant Fernando Sánchez-Arjona scored another shootdown:

> I took off with Escalante when they gave us the alarm of enemy aircraft. It was not difficult to find them: there were about fifteen LaGG-5s, which seemed to be on a free fighter mission. We had just finished protecting some Henschel Hs 126 reconnaissance planes and we were not short of fuel, so we did not hesitate to launch ourselves at them. I was lucky in this fight, because I dived at high speed, trying to surprise them. When I was at about 700 km/h, the plane I was attacking saw me turning immediately at very low speed. I thought I was eating it, because of the speed difference, so I fired a very short burst in a difficult position. The plane went into a tailspin and crashed …[5]

On 5 August, when the Spanish flew three sorties each, Lieutenant Sánchez-Arjona, as leader, and Ensign Aldecoa, as point man, were on reconnaissance duty protecting an Fw 189. At the end of the service and upon their return to the field, they saw two LaGG-5s and a LaGG-3. The veteran of the 3rd Squadron, Aldecoa, went after them and, in a few minutes, managed to shoot down the two LaGG-5s, achieving his first double, reaching five victories and obtaining ace status.

The following day saw a new series of combats in which the 4th Squadron achieved six new victories. At 05:00, Lieutenant Sánchez-Arjona (No.5) and Ensign Aldecoa (No.24) took off from the Prost field for a new protection of an Hs 126 that was to reconnoitre the movements of the Russian troops during the night. This type of service was not to the liking of the Spanish pilots due to the great differences in speed between the two types of aircraft, which meant that they had to make constant swerves over the Hs 126 in order to not lose sight of it. But luck favoured them when seven LaGG-3s and five LaGG-5s appeared and tried to prevent the service. Sánchez-Arjona went after a LaGG-3 and shot it down after a few shots. For his part, Aldecoa went for another without noticing that it was over enemy territory and at a very dangerous altitude. And so, at the very moment he managed to shoot it down, the explosion of a 76.2mm anti-aircraft shell hit Aldecoa, tearing off his depth rudder and right tail empennage. He was also hit in the propeller and fuselage. It is unquestionable that only good luck prevented the Fw 190 A-3 from going into an uncontrolled tailspin. Aldecoa, who knew very well how his plane was doing, took altitude, and, once he considered that he was safe, he launched the canopy to prepare for a forced landing. However, as No.24 was still flying, he decided to continue, managing to reach the field and land normally.

Also on that day, Ensign Javier Mª Guibert, another 3rd Squadron attaché, managed to shoot down a LaGG-5, while his pair leader, Lieutenant Francisco Valiente, managed a double by shooting down two more LaGG-5s:

> I was protecting He 111s, with Guibert as wingman, who had to turn back when his oxygen mask did not work. I was higher up than the bombers, towards the sun, I remember the intensity of the offensive towards the Spas-Demensk–Moscow road, as all the supplies were going that way. We knew of the existence of an enemy airfield over the sector and it was almost passing through the vertical (the latter belonged to the French Normandie-Niemen Squadron). I warped up and saw them taking off, so I dived for one. I was inexperienced and my nerves made me shoot from a distance that was not advisable, but I hit it with a burst that cut its left plane. He could not parachute out. I went back to gain altitude and went for the next one, which I did not see fall, but the He 111s did. I soon ran out of weapons, but I kept attacking, as it is known that from below they were saying: 'Look out, you have got one on your tail!' And they fled right away. If I had been an experienced pilot, I could have shot down up to four aircraft …[6]

Finally, flying over the same area, Lieutenant Bernardo Meneses spotted a formation of 10 LaGG-5s being guided by a Pe-2, immediately positioned himself over the Pe-2 and shot it down with an accurate burst. This Pe-2 was what the Russians called a '*Shturman*', which meant that it was the guide for the fighter groups heading to the front to fight.

The next day, Lieutenant Dámaso Arango encountered four LaGG-5s, which he attacked. He was fortunate enough to hit one of them, which plummeted and crashed to the ground.

On 8–9 August, fighting resumed, but luck was not on the Spaniards' side, and no shootdowns were achieved.

5 Arráez Cerdá, 'Les Espagnols de la Luftwaffe', 19, p.13.
6 Arráez Cerdá, 'Les Espagnols de la Luftwaffe', 19, p.14.

On 10 August, Lieutenant Sánchez-Arjona engaged LaGG-3s and managed to shoot one down. However, in an oversight, he was hit by fire from another LaGG-3 and was forced to parachute out, falling onto his own lines and returning to service a few days later. In the same engagement, the pair of Ensigns Aldecoa and Guibert, both veterans of the 3rd Squadron, were again lucky and managed to shoot down a LaGG-3 each.

The following day, two more victories over LaGG-3s were achieved by Lieutenants Meneses and Sánchez-Tabernero.

In the second half of August, the 4th Squadron achieved a respectable 25 shootdowns but unfortunately at a high price, as they lost three of their pilots: two KIA and a third seriously wounded.

At 04:45 on 12 August, the first two alarm patrols took off. The first was composed of Captain Ozores and Lieutenant Valiente, and the second of Lieutenant Sánchez-Tabernero and Ensign Aldecoa. Both were ordered to protect a group of He 111s that were to bomb over the Kirow sector. Lieutenant Valiente recalled the combat many years later:

> I was going with Ozores as a partner when we came across two LaGG-5s, which did not refuse to fight. It did not take me long to get on the tail of the first one, but I could see that his partner was catching my tail and, at the same time, I could hear Ozores behind him. It was a full-fledged whiting. I was in tremendous doubt, as I had the LaGG-5 almost in range, but I was sure that, if I continued for a few more seconds, I would be the one to fall, so I dedicated myself to removing the one behind me. It was not easy. We started to tack downhill and I could always see him on my tail; in one manoeuvre, I managed to throw him off and I decided to return to the field. But I had a bad taste in my mouth, so I put the engine in, got some altitude and returned to the place of the fight. I was surprised to find my opponent there. This time I was lucky: I shot him down and watched him parachute out ...[7]

The other pair managed to shoot down two LaGG-5s, one by Sánchez-Tabernero and the other by Aldecoa, the latter being Aldecoa's last win in Russia.

Later, at 06:35, Captain Llaca and Lieutenant Lucas took off to protect a Fw 189 that was to reconnoitre and photograph the damage done by the He 111s. LaGG-3s tried to attack the Fw 189, but the Spanish pair intervened, and combat ensued. '*Pepe*' Llaca managed to shoot down one of them.

Captain Llaca running to his aircraft during an alarm. Each alarm patrol had two aircraft ready for immediate take-off. The state of the airfield during the winter period is clearly visible.

7 Arráez Cerdá, 'Les Espagnols de la Luftwaffe', 19, p.15.v

But the toughest combat was the one fought by Lieutenants Lorenzo Lucas Fernández-Peña, Gerardo Escalante de la Lastra and Diego Vigueras Murube. According to Lieutenant Lucas:

> We went out to perform a free fighter service. Captain Galarza was in command, but during the taxiing he got a flat tyre and ordered me to command the formation. We were below the cloud ceiling when, suddenly, we saw a German reconnaissance aircraft dive sharply, which led us to believe that it was being pursued by Russians. I broke through the clouds to intercept them and spotted them higher and to the right. I sounded the alarm and, taking advantage of the sun, took up an advantageous position. Once overhead, I gave the attack signal and decided to stay and protect the pair …[8]

Lieutenant Gerardo Escalante de la Lastra continued the story:

> I launched myself at one, firing. The pilot of the LaGG, feeling attacked, straightened up his plane, turning left. Given my superior speed, I closed the distance and continued firing until I shot him down, overtaking him in the attack. I immediately pulled back to take up a new position. As I was slowing down, I felt an explosion in my legs and there was a burst of fire that reached my clothes. I had no choice: I dropped the canopy and prepared to parachute. The parachute opened without difficulty, but on the way down I saw the LaGG-5 strafing me. In an unconscious attempt, I tried to tackle it with my pistol, but I could do nothing, as my hands were burnt and I could not mount it. I had no choice but to feign death, in order to stop the attack, at the cost of burning myself more. When I reached the ground, in a last effort, I managed to extinguish my clothes. From a nearby village, soldiers began to come and shoot at me, believing that I was the Russian pilot they had just shot down. Then, with the language difficulties, I managed after an hour to be evacuated, as the sector was in full operation and there were many wounded. No doubt I was shot down when the Russian reinforcements arrived and the good Lucas was protecting Vigueras …[9]

When he arrived at the squadron, few believed that Escalante would recover. Only the professionalism and dedication of Medical Captain López Coterilla worked the miracle. Lieutenant Escalante would be a casualty for the rest of the operations. His injuries were truly tremendous, and Juan Arráez (coauthor of this book) can vouch for this, as he had the pleasure and honour of meeting and treating Escalante when he was the colonel-in-chief of Fighter Wing No.11, which flew the Dassault Mirage IIIEE at the unfortunately now defunct Manises Air Base in Valencia. Juan Arráez saw Escalante's injuries in a changing room when they were putting on their flight suits.

While this was happening, the Ju 52 liaison aircraft landed at the airfield, arriving with Captain Álvaro Borras Marimón, Lieutenants Salvador Serra Alorda, Enrique Pareja Núñez and José Cavanilles Bereterra and Ensigns Luis Chicharro Lamamié de Clairac, Luis Estébanez Vela and José Recasens Garriga, who were the members of the third and last expedition of the 4th Squadron.

The arrival of these new pilots was not an obstacle to the continuity of the shootdowns. On 14 August, Captain Galarza shot down a LaGG-5. Two days later, Commander Cuadra, who was flying a free fighter service, was hit by the Russian flak and had to make a forced landing at Katchinina, where he was later rescued by Lieutenant Arango, who was flying a Fieseler Fi 156. On 18 August, four new victories were achieved: an Il-2 and a LaGG-3 by Commander Cuadra, another Il-2 by Captain '*Pepe*' Llaca and a last Il-2 by Lieutenant Dámaso Arango.

The following day, Lieutenant Sánchez-Tabernero managed to shoot down a new Il-2:

> I took off around midday with Ensign Recasens, who had just joined the squadron. It was a free fighter service and, incidentally, to accommodate him a little to the front. When I had been flying for about twenty-five minutes I saw some Il-2s protected by LaGG-5s. They had not seen us. I signalled to the ensign and we dived for the Il-2s. I managed to catch them before they hit the ground, a practice they used to protect themselves. I warned my wingman to be careful, as the Il-2 was a very dangerous aircraft, because of its tail gun. On that day I was lucky enough to fly an Fw 190 A-3 with four guns, and I shot at it with everything I had. I saw it drop a lot of pieces and crash …[10]

The fighting during August was proving exhausting for the Spanish, who barely had time to rest before starting a new mission. Apart from the 'infinite' planes that the Soviets managed to put into flight, the Soviet anti-aircraft artillery

8 Arráez Cerdá, 'Les Espagnols de la Luftwaffe', 19, p.15.
9 Arráez Cerdá, 'Les Espagnols de la Luftwaffe', 19, p.15.
10 Arráez Cerdá, 'Les Espagnols de la Luftwaffe', 19, pp.16–17.

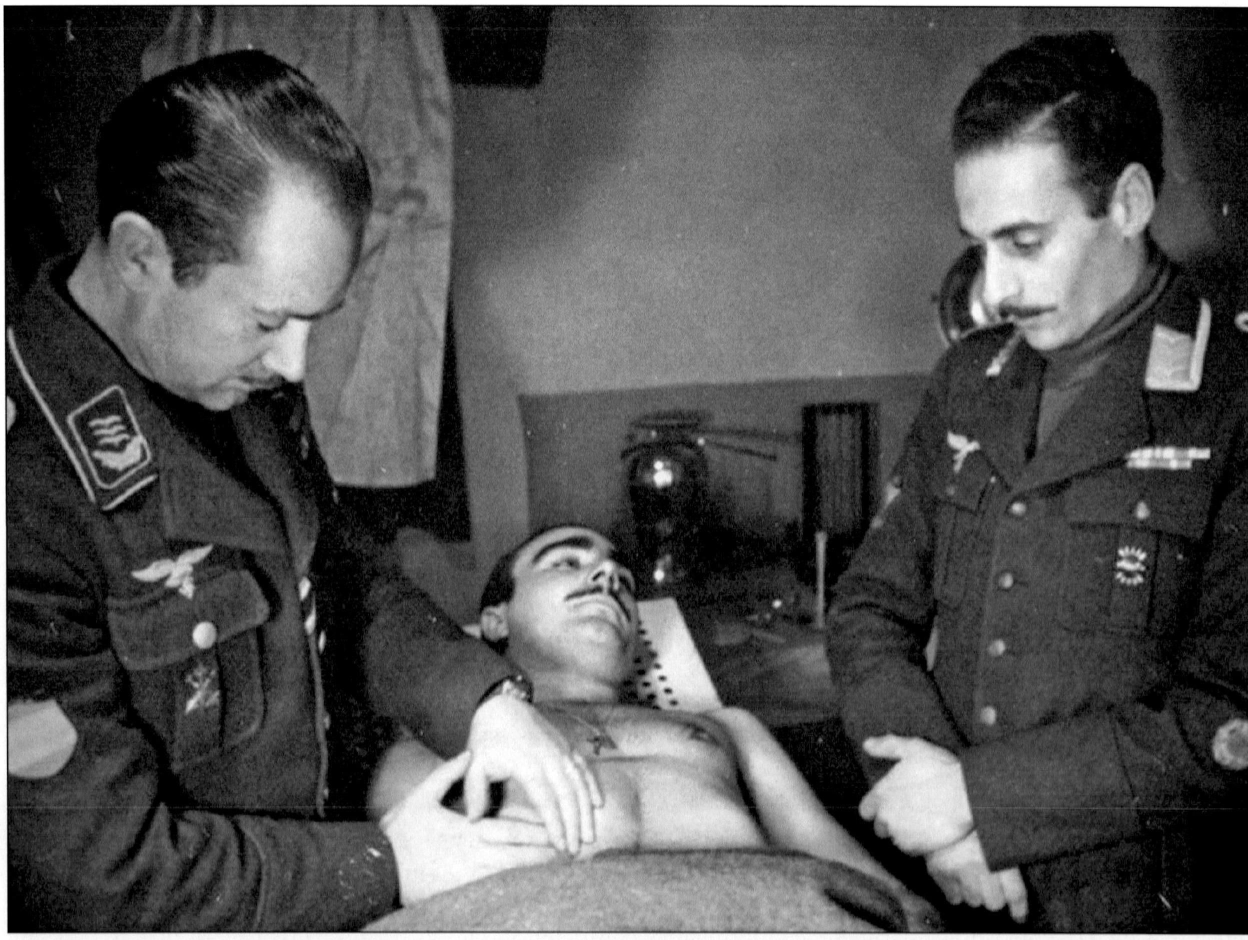

Medical Captain Vicente Lopez Coterilla of the 4th Squadron attending to a patient. As with the entire ground echelon, the medical services played an important role in the smooth running of the various Blue Squadrons.

was becoming more powerful and dangerous by the day. Casualties among the Spanish were mounting, and, of course, among their *Luftwaffe* comrades. The Kharkov front was proving to be a drain on both pilots and aircraft.

On 21 August, the 4th Squadron lost its second pilot in combat: Ensign Luis Chicharro Lamamié de Clairac. At 15:00, Ensign Chicharro took off in the white Fw 190 A-2 No.5 as Commander Cuadra's point, and, five minutes later, another pair, consisting of Captain Borrás and Lieutenant Arango, took off for a free fighter service in the same sector. As the first pair flew over Spas-Demensk, they engaged in combat with the usual LaGG-3s and LaGG-5s, as well as some Yak-9s. Ensign Chicharro went into a tailspin but came out of it under the cloud cover and disappeared from the view of the commander, who, bearing in mind that it was the ensign's first combat, ordered him by radio to return to the airfield. Either he did not hear the order or, driven by his spirit, decided to continue the fight. Meanwhile, Major Cuadra was being harassed by three Soviet fighters, which had hit him and caused one of the legs of his plane's landing gear to deploy. When it seemed that his fate was sealed, Captain Borrás and Lieutenant Arango appeared and took the Russians off his back, enabling him to return to the base safely. There, shortly afterwards, a communication was received from a German flak battery stating that, at 15:25, they had observed a collision between a Fw 190 and a LaGG-5 near Nikolskoje, which crashed 10km inside enemy lines without any observed parachute drops. Since only Spanish aircraft were in the air at the time, it was confirmed that the Fw 190 was that of Ensign Chicharro. In the battle, Galarza shot down a LaGG-5, and Arango a LaGG-3.

The overflowing joy of the day due to the departure to Spain of the last members of the 3rd Squadron, as well as that of Lieutenant Diego Vigueras Murube, who was leaving because of disagreements with Commander Mariano Cuadra, was marred by the death of the young ensign. They left on 22 August in the Ju 52 liaison plane, bound for Berlin and piloted by Lieutenants Calvo and Rego.

On 24 August, Lieutenant Sánchez-Tabernero managed to shoot down another Il-2:

> It was my first encounter with Russian bombers, which I was already doubting they existed. I attacked two '*Vacas*' ['Cows', as the Spanish called the Il-2s] protected by eight LaGG-3s. My point man was '*Pepín*' Cavanilles, who had joined the squadron shortly before. I attacked one of them from the tail, *Pepín* guarding

Major Mariano Cuadra Medina has just returned from a service in which he had achieved a new victory. In total, he achieved 10 confirmed shootdowns – six LaGG-3s, two Il-2s, one LaGG-5 and one Bell P-39 Airacobra – obtaining the Iron Cross 2nd Class and the Spanish Military Medal.

> my back. I was lucky and after the first few cannon shots it crashed without having offered any resistance. The fighters, which were flying above us, did not make the slightest sign of attacking us, probably because they did not see us, as we were much lower and it was not easy to distinguish a camouflaged aircraft when it has the terrain as a background ...[11]

The tasks of the squadron's aircraft were repeated day after day, although sometimes different tasks were carried out. On 27 August, a Blue Squadron patrol consisting of four pilots and their aircraft was sent to Smolensk, where the HQ of JG 51 *Mölders* and the *Stukas* units commanded by the then Major Hans Ulrich Rudel were located. The pilots were Captain Borrás, Lieutenant Sánchez-Tabernero and Ensigns Estébanez Vela and Mateo Recio. Also on that day, '*Perico*' Lacalle left in the Ju 52 for a connection to a Spanish hospital in Berlin, as he had been wounded for a month.

A day later, five shootdowns were achieved. Lieutenant Arango shot down an Il-2, thus achieving ace status by reaching five victories. In addition, Major Cuadra and Lieutenant Sánchez-Arjona had taken off for free fighters, and they had combat with LaGG-3s, of which Cuadra shot down two and Sánchez-Arjona one. The last victory of the day was achieved by Lieutenant Enrique Pareja Núñez, who shot down an Il-2.

On 29 August, there were two more victories, as Captain José '*Pepe*' Llaca and Lieutenant José Cavanilles each shot down a LaGG-5.

On 31 August, JG 51 HQ gave the order for all pilots, German and Spanish, to be ready to perform free fighter and bomber protection services, as the enemy infantry advance had to be stopped at all costs. The first patrol to take off consisted of Major Cuadra and Lieutenants Arjona, Valiente and Pareja. Shortly after, when they were in sight of the He 111 they were to protect, an enemy fighter appeared. Major Cuadra quickly launched himself at the LaGG-3 and smashed its right wing with a barrage from the four guns of his Fw 190 A-3, but he had come too close, and one of the detached pieces

11 Arráez Cerdá, 'Les Espagnols de la Luftwaffe', 19, p.18.

The white Focke-Wulf Fw 190 A-2 No.12 of Lieutenant Cavanilles.

of the LaGG-3 hit his aircraft, damaging it. He tried to return to base, but, unable to get there, he made an emergency landing at the Chatalowska airfield.

While this was going on, Lieutenant Cavanilles, who was on free fighter duty, had engaged in combat and managed to shoot down another LaGG-3.

At Smolensk, the detached patrol had fought LaGG-3s and LaGG-5s in the morning to no avail and then, at 12:00, was ordered to return to the Seschtchinskaja field and, along the way, escort a formation of Ju 88s that were to bomb in the Jelnja area. At 12:45, with Captain Borrás and Ensign Mateos as a pair to be followed by Lieutenant Sánchez-Tabernero and Ensign Estébanez as another, Lieutenant Sánchez-Tabernero's Fw 190 had its engine cowling come open. The lieutenant returned to the line to have it closed, and he told the captain that it was only a minute and to wait for him, but Captain Borrás replied that he was taking off and that the meeting point would be with the Ju 88s. When the first pair was already with the Ju 88s, a large number of enemy fighters appeared. Captain Borrás began the attack, followed by Ensign Mateos, who quickly shot down a LaGG-3 and then lost sight of the captain as he could not distinguish him among the many planes in the sky. Ensign Mateos called him on the radio without getting an answer and then, being short of fuel, continued to Seschtchinskaja. Captain Borrás had been shot down, and his plane had crashed at 13:19 in grid 35371, in no man's land. When an attempt was subsequently made to recover his body, it was impossible, as the front line had changed and he was a few kilometres inside enemy lines.

Thus ended the month of August, which was otherwise the most glorious of all the Blue Squadrons. In the heavy fighting of the later known Battle of Orel, a total of 640 war services were performed, with 121 engagements and 44 aircraft shot down, even at the price of two killed, one missing and two seriously wounded.

The month of September began with Captain Llaca shooting down his fourth aircraft: an Il-2. The following three days, no shootdowns were achieved. On 4 September, Lieutenant Sánchez-Tabernero had an engine failure and had to make an emergency take-off, with the train inside, just before reaching the runway head. He was injured and had a broken eyebrow, so he had no choice but to spend a week without being able to fly.

On 5 September, Captain Cuadra and Lieutenant Arjona went out once again on their second duty of the day: a free fighter mission over the Jelnja sector, where they encountered Russian fighters. They engaged in combat with two LaGG-5s and two American-made Bell P-39 Airacobras, the first time they had fought against this type of aircraft. As a result, Arjona managed to shoot down a LaGG-5.

Two days later, on 7 September, the same pilots came across a formation of nine Il-2s and went after them, shooting down one each and taking their individual tallies to eight victories. Behind them was another pilot who did not want to

At the Smolensk airfield, one of the Fw 190s of the 4th Squadron is unable to stop in time and is mounted on another, which would be permanently lost.

be left behind, Lieutenant Lorenzo Lucas Fernández-Peña, who, on the same day, scored his sixth victory by attacking and shooting down a LaGG-3.

The Russian advance continued, unstoppable, and their outposts were very close to Bryansk, which fell to them on 14 September. Before then, on 9 September, the 4th Squadron was already ordered to abandon the airfield and move to the Smolensk airfield. Consequently, most of the specialists left in German Ju 52s, and the troops left at night in a column of trucks.

The next day, the Fw 190s began to take off for Smolensk in patrols, although the remaining pilots and specialists first went to the cemetery to pray for their fallen comrades, whose graves they would never see again. Once the Fw 190s had taken off, the few remaining specialists gathered their belongings and, in a Ju 52, left for the Smolensk field.

During the flight, Lieutenant Arjona found an opportunity to shoot down a LaGG-5, thus obtaining his ninth and last shootdown in the USSR. He was flying, as usual, with Commander Cuadra.

On 12 September, there was another shootdown, not of an aircraft but of a captive observation balloon that was well protected by a good anti-aircraft defence and fighters. According to Lieutenant Valiente:

> I flew a lot with Serra, who was older than me and with whom I had a good friendship. For some reason, although he was supposed to fly as the leader, he preferred to fly as a point man and that I was the one who led the formation. Even if more of us had to go and Serra was in command, he always put me in charge, even if there were other pilots older than me. That day we flew into enemy territory at high altitude; making a detour we headed for the place where the balloon was. Its defenders, seeing us coming from their own lines and with the sun behind us, mistook us for theirs and, before they could react, we strafed the balloon …[12]

No more shootdowns could be obtained until 15 September, when, during a Ju 87 protection service in the Jelnja sector, eight Fw 190s took off under Commander Cuadra since, as usual, he never missed a service. During the flight, they encountered four Airacobras and three LaGG-5s, and the commander managed to shoot down one of each model, beating his 'competitor' Lieutenant Arjona. In a following service, Lieutenant Arango shot down a Pe-2, thus reaching six victories.

12 Arráez Cerdá, 'Les Espagnols de la Luftwaffe', 19, p.19.

On 17 September, there was a lot of fighting, as the Soviets had begun to enter the city of Bryansk and the Germans had begun the counterattack, supporting their infantry with numerous formations of *Stukas* and the Spaniards in charge of protecting them. Lieutenant Sánchez-Tabernero recalled:

> The service on the morning of the 17th was undoubtedly the one I enjoyed most of the whole campaign. I took off with Serra, Mateos and Valiente, in a patrol that I commanded, with the order to protect a formation of Junkers Ju 87s. There were a lot of clouds and we flew towards the front, entering and leaving them at a low altitude, because if we went in any higher we would definitely get in and get lost. We had been flying for quite a while and I reckoned that we must have been close to the '*Stukas*', when as I came out into the clearing between the fringes of a cloud I found myself within range of a formation of twelve or fifteen Il-2s [*Vacas*] and some LaGGs around them. All I had to do was to fire on the nearest bomber and, even better, in the first burst I blew up the ammunition tank, which was in the cigar socket with the plane, sending up a huge flare and sending the plane crashing to the ground in a few seconds. Serra was congratulating me on the downing, when I was already on the tail of another '*Vaca*', which, although it took a little longer to do so, also crashed in a slow turn. I had done a double, something I had never dreamed of. We had swallowed the formation from below and I flew back close to the ground, but when I tried to make contact with the planes again I did not see them nor the '*Stukas*' anymore. I returned to the field with mine, full of satisfaction …[13]

This satisfaction was shared by Valiente and Mateos since they also shot down an Il-2 each. In addition, in a previous service, Lieutenant Cavanilles had shot down a LaGG-5. With these shootdowns, the 4th Squadron reached the respectable figure of 70 victories.

By the end of 17 September, the Soviets definitively conquered Bryansk and continued their advance, which meant that Smolensk and its airfield were in danger of falling into their hands. The Germans therefore began to prepare to blow up their hangars and installations at the slightest presence of Russian troops. The 4th Squadron was ordered to evacuate the airfield and head for the Orsha field; only a couple of Fw 190s and a small group of specialists remained operating there until the last moment.

A day later, it was necessary to escort Hs 126 reconnaissance and He 111 bombardment aircraft. To do this, a pair formed by Captain Llaca and Ensign Estébanez was appointed, followed by another of Lieutenant Sánchez-Tabernero and Ensign Mateos. Once the service ended without incident, they started their return, and, shortly after, Llaca gave warning of enemy fighters. With Estébanez at his side, they headed towards them, verifying that they were three LaGG-3s. The Russians saw them and tried to escape in two directions, so the Spanish pair went after the one escaping to the west. Llaca opened fire, catching up with it and watching as it began to billow white smoke and drift into the sea of clouds. He lost sight of it, and, at that moment, Llaca realised that his wingman had disappeared. The *Wehrmacht* observation posts reported that they had seen a battle in this sector between Fw 190s and enemy fighters, witnessing the downing of one of them, without being able to say whether it was their own or the enemy's, and seeing a pilot descend in a parachute, whom the wind carried into enemy lines. Nothing more was heard of Ensign Estébanez Vela, who was reported missing in action (MIA).

In those days, the Russians had a large number of Yak-9s at their disposal, and, although the Spanish already had quite a few Fw 190 A-3s, they were inferior to the Yak-9. Only the skill and experience of the Spanish pilots meant that there were no more casualties.

On 20 September, the pair formed by Lieutenants Sánchez-Tabernero and Valiente met the Yak-9s for the first time, and Valiente was about to be shot down, as he recounted:

> I took off with Sánchez-Tabernero to protect a '*Súper Pava*' ['super female turkey', the name by which the Spanish called the Hs 126 since the time of the GCE]. Soon after, we saw a Pe-2 and decided to go for it; we realised that it was carrying fighter protection; they were Yak-9s, the famous plane we had heard so much about. I had never had a problem getting anyone off my tail before, but this time it was different.[14]

Lieutenant Sánchez-Tabernero continued the story:

> I engaged one of them nose to nose, as if we were doing a combat drill at school or in any unit. In this first encounter I knew what this plane was like; it had immediately gained altitude on me and soon after I was at its expense. It had me with its nose high off the vertical and about to stall, and to prevent it from getting on my tail I had no choice but to turn around at a moment when the sun was in my favour, trying to get away from that monster as fast as I could.

13 Arráez Cerdá, 'Les Espagnols de la Luftwaffe', 19, p.22.

14 Arráez Cerdá, 'Les Espagnols de la Luftwaffe', 19, p.22.

> When I regained position, I saw, far and higher, three aircraft fighting and I assumed that one would be Valiente. I manoeuvred away while gaining altitude to enter them at my convenience and with overspeed. I heard Valiente calling for arnica, saying he had two on his tail ...[15]

And that was indeed the case. According to Valiente's account:

> When I turned my neck I saw two Yaks stuck to me, and I heard Manolo say to me: 'You have them on you, you have them on you!' I looked again and saw with astonishment that there were not two but three, which I exclaimed in desperation over the radio. But for my little peace of mind, Manolo shouted to me: 'The third one is me, go flat out or they will shoot you down!' I put the throttle all the way in, going vertical and at about 800 km/h, but they would not come off; I could see tracers go by and I noticed that something came off the engine and hit the tail; I thought they had shot me down. I pulled into the sun and blinded myself, thinking that if they did it, at least they would not be able to see me. When I levelled the plane I checked that no one was following me and returned to the base. I think that I must have lost two kilos in that fight and my heart must have aged four years ...[16]

The Spanish pilots had just seen how the Yak-9s, which, in this case, most likely belonged to the Normandie-Niemen Squadron, were used by the enemy. Encounters with Yak-9s began to become more frequent, which made it very difficult for the Spaniards to shoot them down due to the excellent characteristics of the Russian aircraft.

On 22 September, the last remaining Spaniards left Smolensk, and, three days later, the Russians entered the city. Precisely on that day, the 4th Squadron was ordered to move to the Stara Bychow, or Stra.Bychov, camp, using the Orsha camp only as a temporary one.

The month of September ended without any other news worthy of mention. A total of 518 war services had been performed in this month, with 58 combats and 15 shootdowns, at the cost of the loss of Ensign Luis Estébanez Vela.

Throughout this period of withdrawal, there were no further Spanish victories despite the continuous flying of missions and the presence of numerous Soviet aircraft. Finally, the Soviet advance was halted by the Germans in the central zone of the Russian front in October, so there was a short period of time in which the Spanish pilots could rest after the maelstrom of the previous months. But the Axis situation was worsening on all fronts, and Spain's political and strategic situation definitely made it a possible Allied target. Spain was already forced by Allied pressure to withdraw the Blue Division from Russia, and, of course, the Blue Squadron was soon to suffer the same fate (the presence of Spanish pilots in the *Luftwaffe* was not as widespread as that of the Blue Division soldiers).

The central front stabilised at the end of September, and the Russian offensive shifted to the southern sector. This, together with a worsening of the weather, meant that the squadron's flying activity was considerably reduced. Given the heavy exhaustion suffered by the pilots, this drop in activity was a good opportunity for them to recuperate, as their leader, Commander Cuadra, ordered them to leave in pairs in the Ju 52 liaison for Berlin for a week of relaxation.

On 12 October, the feast of the Virgin of the Pillar, the patroness of Spain, a serious incident occurred that fortunately did not cause any casualties. At 09:15, Ensign José Recasens Garriga was ordered to take off immediately due to an alarm over the field. When he was at an altitude of 6,000m, he was ordered to join Lieutenant Lorenzo Lucas Fernández-Peña, who had taken off with Lieutenants Dámaso Arango López and José Cavanilles Bereterra, although the latter had to return to the field due to a breakdown 10 minutes into the flight. Recasens took off and joined his comrades. When they reached the front line, they came up against a layer of clouds that were at a lower altitude; Lucas then ordered a slow descent to cross it. Just then, Lieutenant Lorenzo Lucas heard Ensign Recasens say that he had slack in the controls of his plane, so he ordered him to return immediately to the airfield. Recasens continued for a few moments with his comrades, who were starting a climb and suddenly saw him start a dive to the left and something break away. It was the canopy of the Fw 190 followed by Ensign Recasens, who, when he jumped in a dive, hit the rudder but fortunately had already pulled the ring and the parachute opened perfectly. His comrades, who were flying around him as he fell, saw his limp body and feared the worst, but fortunately this was not the case. He was immediately picked up by a German patrol, and it was found that he had only suffered a broken left leg, so he was discharged for the rest of the campaign and returned to Spain shortly afterwards.

In the following days, services continued without incident until 21 October, when an order was received to intercept eight Il-2s and LaGG-3s. Captain Felipe Galarza and Lieutenants Lorenzo Lucas, Enrique Pareja and '*Pepín*' Cavanilles, who was on standby, quickly took off. Barely 10 minutes had elapsed when *Pepín* reported that his engine had broken down, so the captain ordered him to return. Forty minutes later, Lieutenant Lucas also suffered an engine failure and was forced to return. This showed the exhaustion suffered by the Fw 190s flown by the Spaniards. When Galarza and Pareja

15 Arráez Cerdá, 'Les Espagnols de la Luftwaffe', 19, p.22.
16 Arráez Cerdá, 'Les Espagnols de la Luftwaffe', 19, p.22.

had been flying for an hour and a quarter, the captain decided to land at the Orsha field to refuel. While there, they were given an order to take off in a free fighter over the eastern sector of Orsha, so they took off at 14:00, heading north.

As they flew over the Orsha–Moscow highway, at 2,000m, Lieutenant Pareja warned of anti-aircraft fire to the right, about 100m away. Captain Galarza turned there and left Pareja a little behind him on the left. At that moment, the lieutenant warned his captain of enemy aircraft to the right and indicated that he was losing sight of them because of the haze, but the captain realised that they were two pairs of Il-2s coming at him head-on. He dived at the first of them, and, when he was on their tail, he heard his point tell him, 'You have a fighter on your tail'. Looking back, the captain saw with astonishment that they were Yak-9s and immediately gave a jerk. When he recovered, he saw that there was a fairly large engagement to the south. He gained altitude and tried to catch the sun, soon seeing a burning aircraft on the ground but not what type it was. Later, the 4th Squadron reported that the wreckage belonged to Lieutenant Enrique Pareja's Fw 190 No.8. His body was recovered and subsequently buried in the Orsha field cemetery with the corresponding military honours.

Two new victories were achieved on 29 October: the first when Lieutenant Arango shot down an Il-2, thus achieving his seventh and last shootdown and with it his Military Medal (*Medalla Militar*), and the second by Lieutenant Cavanilles, who, on free fighter service, flying his usual Fw 190 No.12, shot down another Il-2, his fourth and last victory in the USSR. Also on that day, Ensign Lago, in command of his group of specialists, went to the Orsha field in a German Ju 52.

Lieutenant Dámaso Arango López, one of the pilots of the 4th Squadron with seven victories, in flight uniform showing his Iron Cross on his chest.

In this unfruitful month of October, 333 war services were performed, with 22 engagements, and only two victories were achieved at the cost of two pilots. One was killed, and the other seriously wounded.

The month of November saw the arrival of the harsh Russian winter, as snow began to make its appearance along with the cold and dark days. This month also got off to a bad start: when Major Cuadra was in Orsha inspecting the Il-2 shot down by Lieutenant Arango, he slipped with such bad luck that he broke his leg and had to be evacuated to a hospital in Berlin on 10 November in the Ju 52 liaison plane. Galarza, who had just been promoted to major, was appointed to replace him.

In the first fortnight of the month, there were hardly any flights. On 17 November, although the weather was really hellish, a patrol was ordered to leave to protect an Hs 126 in the Orsha sector. The protection was carried out without problems by Lieutenants Lorenzo Lucas, Fernando Sánchez-Arjona and Salvador Serra and Ensign José Mateos.

They then refuelled at Orsha, but, when they were preparing to take off to return to their base, they were forced to delay their flight due to a severe deterioration in the weather. As a result, they were forced to spend the rest of the day there, tediously and boringly, in addition to lacking the most basic necessities. Because of this and their friendship with Lucas, the three other pilots of the patrol pressed him to return to their camp in Stara Bychow the next morning. Thus, at 06:15, the four Fw 190s took off from Orsha. The first pair consisted of Lieutenants Lorenzo Lucas and Fernando Sánchez-Arjona, and the second of Lieutenant Salvador Serra and Ensign José Mateos. Lucas' orders were very clear: under no circumstances were the others to be separated from him, and, if he decided to return, they would all do so together. Once in the air, instead of turning south (the direct course to Stara Bychow), the first pair stayed in the direction of their take-off, heading east for about four kilometres then turning north in order to take the 270-degree turn necessary to set course for their airfield. During this manoeuvre, Lieutenant Lucas observed that, about six kilometres south of the field, where the forest area began, a fog barrier formed that filled the clearing between the ground and clouds. This barrier, however, allowed them to continue in low-level flight. But before reaching it, Lucas noticed ice forming on his windscreen, so he immediately turned and ordered the second pair, whom he could not see, to return to Orsha's field. When Lucas was over the airfield, he heard his partner, Lieutenant Sánchez-Arjona, say something he could not understand. Once on the ground, he telephoned the Stara Bychow field, where he was informed of the safe arrival of the second pair, whose pilots had neither seen nor heard the first pair, as they assumed that they were ahead of them. Almost at the same time, Lucas received word that, six kilometres south of the airfield, a plane was on fire. It was Lieutenant Fernando Sánchez-Arjona's

Three Spanish pilots of the 4th Squadron pose for the photographer in front of a Fieseler Fi 156. From left to right: Lieutenants Pareja (who was shot down on 21 October 1943), Arango and Fernández-Peña.

One of the Spanish pilots poses next to the wreckage of a Soviet plane shot down by the 4th Blue Squadron.

Lieutenant Fernando Sánchez Arjona Courtoy, who, with nine victories, died on 19 November 1943 when his Fw 190 A-2 crashed due to an ice formation shortly after taking off from the Orsha airfield.

Fw 190, which had been grounded by the ice formation, ending the life of what many considered to be the best fighter in the 4th Squadron.

From Stara Bychow, Lieutenants Sánchez-Tabernero and '*Pepín*' Cavanilles, together with *Pater* Captain Gonzalo de los Ríos, travelled in the Fieseler Fi 156 *Storch* assigned to the squadron. Once there, and with the honours of ordinance, the body of Lieutenant Fernando Sánchez-Arjona Courtoy was buried in the Orsha cemetery.

In the following days, the Russian advance continued in the Spanish sector, and consequently the airfield had to be changed again, as Manuel Sánchez-Tabernero recalled:

> On the 24th, in the evening, I went with Dámaso Alonso to the base's cinema and, halfway through the film, the lights came on. A German *Unteroffizier* came on stage and made a speech. I asked Dámaso: 'What is he saying?' and his reply was: 'that there is nothing between us and the Russians'. We went to the pavilions to wait for the orders, which were: 'Transfer to the Bobruisk airfield at dawn'.
>
> First thing in the morning, the pilots who were at the base went to the line.
>
> I seem to remember that there were only six of us, as Commander Cuadra was in Berlin, Captain Llaca was on leave and Galarza was leaving with the ground echelon, so I was the most senior and it was my turn to command the formation. The bad weather was constant and that morning there was a lot of fog, when we most needed to get out of the quagmire we were in. Patience, I said to myself, we cannot rush things because they could easily go wrong.
>
> After 11:00, the fog started to lift a little. It looked better and I decided to take advantage of the small loophole, praying to all the saints in case it closed again.
>
> I gave the order to go out with wings as close together as possible, by seniority, and not to separate for anything in the world. I feared that if the formation broke up in that thick fog there would be a hecatomb, for we would each land in a different place and probably off the field. We took off and the order was carried out to the letter; flying close together and over the treetops, we were able to maintain the formation and, after one of the most bitter moments of my life, visibility increased and we were able to get out of that trap, encountering sunshine and flies. My breath and thanks to God cannot be explained, and I suppose neither can that of my companions; then it was not long before we found ourselves in the Bobruisk vertical, where the Berezina River flows through and where Napoleon's '*Grande Armée*' [Great Army] had its greatest setback in its retreat from Russia.
>
> Let us knock on wood, because something similar could have happened to six Spanish aviation officers …[17]

17 Arráez Cerdá, 'Les Espagnols de la Luftwaffe', 19, p.25.

Captain Llaca of the 4th Squadron posing with his skis in front of an Me 323 at the Bobruisk airfield.

Activity in the month of November decreased considerably, as only 112 services could be carried out, without any shoot-downs, and two pilots were lost: Lieutenant Fernando Sánchez-Arjona, killed, and Ensign José Recasens, wounded. In short: the 4th Squadron had reached a 50 percent loss of its men.

The new Bobruisk airfield was well organised, with many buildings that housed all the personnel stationed there, and what was even better: it had central heating.

In December, services continued to be reduced, as the weather was terrible and the ground was covered with a thick layer of snow. The cold was raging, and it was barely possible to spend a few minutes outdoors. But, despite the few services that were carried out, Lieutenant Francisco Valiente Zárraga had the opportunity to attack a Douglas Boston bomber, which he managed to shoot down.

On 10 December, *Kommodore* Nordmann took advantage of the occasion to visit the Spaniards on the day of their patron saint and, incidentally, to award some Iron Crosses to deserving pilots. On 11 December, Commander Cuadra arrived, now recovered, and resumed command. However, four days later, he gave his men another scare, as he was forced to land to the east of the field due to a breakdown and in not very good conditions, but he was only slightly wounded.

By the end of the year, the 4th Squadron was totally exhausted, and there was not a pilot who had not made several forced overflights due to enemy fire. Russian air superiority was unbelievable. But fortunately, their relief by the 5th Squadron, which had already finished its training period at the St-Jean-d'Angély air base, was scheduled for 9 January 1944.

On the planned day, the Spanish Ju 52, carrying the first patrol of the 5th Squadron (Captain Arróniz, Lieutenants Gil and Vega and Ensigns Tassara and Orúe), landed at the Bobruisk airfield. The replacement of the 4th Squadron was beginning to become a reality. Between 19–22 January 1944, the Spanish Ju 52 carried out its last liaison mission and was no longer used to support the 5th Blue Squadron, as the Spanish government had already taken the decision to repatriate from the front all the Spanish volunteers fighting in the USSR.

On 10 January, the pair of planes piloted by Lieutenants Lucas and Cavanilles took off to protect a formation of Ju 87s, and Lieutenant *'Pepín'* Cavanilles was shot down. This event, coinciding with the presence of the 5th Squadron, will be recounted in the following chapter.

One of the Fw 190 A-3s of the 4th Squadron in winter camouflage. With its four 20mm cannons and two 7.92mm machine guns, the Fw 190 A-3 became a magnificent fighting machine in the hands of the Spanish pilots.

Members of the 4th Blue Squadron during the *rancho*. In the foreground is the officer in charge of tasting the *rancho*.

On 12 January, the last victory by a 4th Squadron pilot was achieved by Lieutenant Valiente when he again shot down a Douglas Boston A-20 Havoc from a formation of seven aircraft, which will also be recounted in the next chapter.

On 16 January, some pilots belonging to the 5th Squadron's advance party began their flights accompanied by veterans of the 4th Squadron.

On 24 January, the first Bf 109 G-6s arrived for the Blue Squadron. The next day, the 5th Squadron's ground crew arrived at the Spanish air base to work alongside the 4th Squadron.

On 29 January, the first men of the 4th Squadron began to be repatriated to Spain. Their arrival in their homeland went unnoticed since, at that time in the Second World War, there was no interest in publicising these men who had fought on the German side.

The Allies continued their pressure on Francisco Franco's Spanish government to withdraw all Spanish combatants from the Eastern Front. In January 1944, US Ambassador Hayes, for the first time,

Lieutenant José Cavanilles Vereterra '*Pepín*' with his white Fw 190 No.12, with which, on 10 January 1944, he was shot down and killed in combat by Yak-9 aircraft possibly belonging to the Normandie-Niemen Squadron.

One of the Spanish pilots making a 'fix' during one of the pauses between missions.

Several soldiers of the 4th Squadron's ground echelon pose for the photographer on a motorbike with a sidecar. In the foreground is E. Demetrio Bravo, who served with the 3rd Squadron and later with the 4th.

explicitly requested the withdrawal of the Blue Squadron. On 18 February, the Spanish government, through Foreign Minister Jordana, asked the German ambassador in Madrid for the withdrawal of the Blue Legion (*Legión Azul*), which was the small unit that had replaced the Blue Division on the Eastern Front, and the Blue Squadron. Only two days later, Adolf Hitler granted permission for the Spaniards to return to their homeland.

Despite Spain's intention to repatriate all its soldiers, on 19 February, a Ju 52 arrived at the Spanish air base with the 2nd Patrol of the 5th Blue Squadron and the unit's commander. A few days later, the men of the ground echelon began their journey to Spain.

On 23 February, the 4th Squadron officially ceased its activity, as stated in the order of the day of that date, signed by Inspector Commander Mariano Cuadra at the Bobruisk airfield:

> Today I hand over the command and inspection of the squadron to Commander Javier Murcia Rubio, in compliance with a superior order. On this occasion I express to all the personnel of the 4th Squadron the pride I feel, whose the memory I will always cherish, of having feared the command of soldiers who have always known how to carry out their duty without taking into account risks or fatigue. To those who fell in battle, our everlasting memory, because they are the example of those who, in their desire to serve their country, wanted to die for it ...[18]

18 Arráez Cerdá, 'Les Espagnols de la Luftwaffe', 19, p.27.

Several pilots talk before the next mission, in which they will again have to face Soviet aircraft. During its tour of duty between July 1943 and January 1944, the 4th Squadron managed to shoot down 74 enemy aircraft.

The 4th Squadron withdrew to Spain on 28 February. The 5th Blue Squadron took over on 24 February 1944 at the Bobruisk airfield, where the 1st and 2nd Patrols had already arrived (the 3rd Patrol would never reach the front). The 4th Blue Squadron, whose ground echelon had arrived in Spain on 22 March, was officially disbanded in Madrid.

The 4th Blue Squadron flew 1,918 combat missions, engaging in 277 dogfights and shooting down 74 aircraft. By the time it withdrew from the front in January 1944, it had lost seven pilots (four officers killed and three missing), to which must be added three seriously wounded, making a casualty rate of 50 percent.

5

5th Squadron

The 5th Blue Squadron was created on 26 October 1943, in Alcalá de Henares, Madrid, following a period of training similar to that received by the pilots of the 4th Squadron, flying CR.32s and Bf 109 Es and advised by Spanish veterans who had fought in Russian skies.

On 28 December, the men of the 1st Patrol of the 5th Squadron took the Oath of Allegiance to the *Führer* for the Eastern Campaign at the French air base of St-Jean-d'Angély.

Several men of the 5th Squadron's ground echelon during their oath of office on 28 December 1943. Behind them is one of the Fw 190s used for training the Spanish pilots.

The training period for the pilots of the 1st Patrol ended on 16 November. Given the situation of the Second World War, the departure of the squadron members to France was carried out almost clandestinely to prevent the Allies from knowing about it. Thus, on 22 November, the 1st Patrol crossed the French border with special security measures and almost secretly in small groups so as not to attract attention (there was fear that the French Resistance might carry out attacks against the Spaniards). The first to cross were Captain Arróniz, an NCO and 10 soldiers, with the 'escort' of Captain '*Pepe*' Llaca, a veteran of the 4th Squadron. Then, it was the turn of the second group, made up of Medical Captain Ayala, Ensign Tassara, an NCO and 10 soldiers. From the Hendaye border, they continued their journey by train to the base at St-Jean-d'Angély, where all the men of the 1st Patrol arrived on 27 November. There, they undertook a month-long training period conducted by the *Luftwaffe* using Fw 190s (which was a bit of a problem for the Spanish pilots and mechanics of the 5th Squadron who used the Bf 109 G-6 in their combat missions). On 27 December, the 1st Patrol completed its training period with Supplementary Fighter Group, South (*Ergänzungs-Jagdgruppe Süd*), and, on 28 December, the men of the 1st Patrol of the 5th Squadron took the Oath of Allegiance to the *Führer* for the Eastern Campaign at the French air base. After a brief stop in Paris, the Spaniards marched to their base, Bobruisk.

An Fw 190 of the 4th Squadron flown by men of the 5th Squadron before the arrival of the Bf 109 G-6s. On 16 January, some pilots belonging to the 5th Squadron advance party began their flights accompanied by veterans of the 4th Squadron. On 24 January, the first Bf 109 G-6s arrived.

Although the 5th Blue Squadron was the last to be sent from Spain to Russia, the commander of the theoretical 6th Blue Squadron, should it be formed, had already been appointed: Major Miguel Guerrero, a veteran of the GCE.

The pilots of the 2nd Patrol of the 5th Blue Squadron departed by train from Madrid, passing the French border completely incognito in three-man groups to avoid detection by Allied espionage (gone were the days when they were greeted with marching bands and big parties as had happened to previous squadrons). In this case, the base to which they were sent was not St-Jean-d'Angély but Bergerac, near Toulouse, where they arrived on 15 January. The training period lasted until 6 February 1944: only 22 days. After a few days in Berlin, the pilots of the first patrol left in the Ju 52 liaison, flown by Lieutenant Cruzate, for the Bobruisk airfield. Captain Isaac Arróniz, Lieutenants Eduardo Vega de Seoane and Esteban Martínez Gil and Ensigns Miguel Tassara Fernández and Jesús Orúe Puga, accompanied by Captain José Llaca and Commander Cárdenas, attached to the Aeronautical Attaché in Berlin, arrived. Later in the afternoon, *Oberstleutnant* Nordmann, *Kommodore* of JG 51, arrived to welcome them.

Another moment of the swearing-in of the 5th Blue Squadron on 28 December 1943, in this case the pilots of the 1st Patrol. Behind them can be seen several Fw 190s.

Lieutenant Esteban Martínez Gil posing with the Ju 52 liaison aircraft that was so necessary for the normal operation of the different Spanish squadrons in the USSR.

The training period in France was not very comfortable for the Spaniards, as Allied air dominance meant that German bases were frequently attacked, making it difficult for the Spaniards to train properly. The relationship with the German instructors was good, as evidenced by the words of the flight instructor responsible for their training, Heinrich Heuser: 'The training lasted until the beginning of February 1944. The pilots had good flying skills, high morale and a great deal of operational complacency. During their stay in *Ergänzungs-Jagdgruppe Süd* they also developed a good relationship with us'.[1]

As mentioned above, the 5th Blue Squadron (1st and 2nd Patrols only) took effect on 23 February 1944 at the Bobruisk airfield. Like the 4th Blue Squadron, the 5th Squadron belonged to JG 51.

The entire 5th Squadron was to consist of a commander-in-chief, 19 pilots, four ground service officers, 11 NCOs and 96 soldiers – making a total of 131 men. This squadron must be considered the least experienced of all those that went to Russia, with only four of the pilots having participated in the GCE. The 5th Squadron was distributed as follows:

1 Neulen, *Skies of Europe*, p.284.

Members of the 5th Squadron pose smiling for the camera during their training period in France next to an Fw 190. It was with this aircraft that they trained, although the Spanish unit was later equipped with the Bf 109 G-6.

The flying conditions for the Bf 109 G-6s of the 5th Squadron were very difficult due to the adverse weather, several degrees below zero.

Staff: Commander-in-Chief Major Murcia
1st Patrol: Captain Arróniz, Lieutenants Gil, Vega, del Río and Segurola and Ensigns Tassara and Orúe
2nd Patrol: Captain Carbó, Lieutenants Alonso, Sacanelles and Maura and Ensign Sanz
3rd Patrol: Captain Díaz, Lieutenant García and Ensigns Salto, Palanca, Cuadra and Gómez.[2]

As mentioned in the previous chapter, on 10 January and with temperatures at minus 12 degrees Celsius, the alarm pair received the warning that they were to leave on escort duty for Ju 87 *Stukas*. For this reason, Lieutenant Lorenzo Lucas, as leader, and Lieutenant José Cavanilles, as point, took off a few minutes after midday, together with six other Fw 190s of the JG 51 HQ Squadron. According to Lucas:

> We took off with six other planes of the German Headquarters Squadron. We were ordered to provide immediate protection while the planes were a little higher up. Over the target we found a large number of Russian aircraft (according to the '*Stukas*', about 150). We avoided several combats so as not to get separated from them and, while they dived to bomb, we took a little more altitude, evading all the attacks they made on us, prepared not to go into action as long as it was not in defence of the '*Stukas*'. José spoke to me and I understood him perfectly, but he always asked me to repeat what I told him. When I saw that the '*Stukas*' were finishing their bombing raids, I told Lieutenant Cavanilles to dive in and protect the exit from the target, attacking the planes below us in the process. When I reached the height of the German bombers, I realised that he was not following me; after a while, he told me that he was in a fight. I told him that I was coming to his aid but to give up, as the enemy superiority was overwhelming. When I was close I was attacked by eight planes. I informed Lieutenant Cavanilles of my plight, telling him to dive hard and head for the field, as I did. At that moment we were in the enemy zone, over grid 9355, south-east of the town of Cawydowitschi ...[3]

Lieutenant '*Pepín*' Cavanilles was the last pilot of the 4th Squadron to be shot down in Russia.

In the last days of service of the 4th Squadron, pilots from the 5th Squadron joined to facilitate the incorporation of the new unit. In the picture is Captain Arróniz of the 5th Squadron (left) and Captain Llaca of the 4th Squadron.

2 This last patrol, as mentioned above, never made it to the front lines, as had also happened to some of the 5th Squadron's ground echelon personnel.
3 Arráez Cerdá, 'Les Espagnols de la Luftwaffe', 19, p.31.

On 12 January 1944, Lieutenant Valiente achieved the last Spanish victory on the Eastern Front:

> That day I was flying as a couple with Lucas. We were alerted to the enemy aircraft alarm and took off. Many times there was an alarm and we did not find anything, but this time it was different. We spotted a formation of seven Douglas 'Bostons' flying in a V and heading for their lines after bombing duty. They were carrying two fighter echelons, the first of which was a thousand metres higher than the bombers. We were at the height of the first echelon. Then they saw us; I was going to dive at them, but Lucas told me to wait. He warped his plane and the Russians responded to us. They must have thought we were one of theirs, because the Fw 190 was very similar to the LaGG-5.
>
> I saw a Douglas pull me into an isolated cloud and, as soon as it came out, I dived for it. As I descended in a steep dive, the whole formation came out of the cloud. When they saw that I was descending on them they started firing at me and also alerted their fighters, which dived for me. The Douglas had one turret above and one below, but it was manned by the same man. Because I had dived vertically, I reached a tremendous speed of about 850 km/h. I thought I was going to crash. I shot from about thirty metres with everything and I hit the jerk. Immediately the Douglas began a rapid wing drop and stalled, its left engine shooting out flames like a blowtorch. It took about ten seconds before it began falling to the ground. The fighters did not attack me, perhaps because Lucas was up there, or because they would be out of gas.[4]

On 13 January, bad weather prevented flights, although some Soviet reconnaissance aircraft were spotted, which was taken as a harbinger of an early start to their offensive.

On 14 January, *Oberstleutnant* Nordmann showed up to tell the Spaniards that they were going to receive new and better aircraft, but it turned out that, instead of being Fw 190s of the latest and best series, they were Bf 109 G-6s, abandoning the Fw 190s that had brought them so many victories. This came as a great surprise, as neither pilots nor mechanics had trained with them, being totally unfamiliar. However, the experience and expertise of the pilots and specialists quickly resolved this difficulty. Very soon, the peculiar idiosyncrasy of the Spaniards christened these new aircraft as '*Chichones*' (Bulges) due to the various bulges in their engine cowlings.

The 5th Blue Squadron was the only one that was able to use the modern German Bf 109 G-6 fighter. Here is one of the Spanish aircraft in winter camouflage ready for take-off, with two men from the Spanish ground echelon as witnesses.

4 Arráez Cerdá, 'Les Espagnols de la Luftwaffe', 19, p.31.

This picture shows the characteristic 'bulge' of the Bf 109 G-6s flown by 5th Squadron pilots. With one 30mm cannon and two 13mm machine guns, this aircraft had less firepower than the Fw 190s of the 4th Squadron.

Although the 5th Squadron pilots had been trained with Fw 190s, they had to quickly get used to their new 'mount', the Bf 109 G-6 (which were not new, as they had previously belonged to other German units). The white runway, due to the snow, is visible.

The cold January days were passing, and the Spanish planes were unable to take off due to the bad weather conditions. In addition, the clear air superiority of the Soviets made any mission a high-risk one. In this regard, the Spanish pilots were ordered not to fly with less than four planes (one patrol) for greater protection.

16 January was one of the first days when the weather allowed flying, and so the pilots of the 5th Squadron took to the air together with the veterans of the 4th Squadron. At 11:00, Lieutenant Serra took off in a pair with Ensign Miguel Tassara Fernández-Barrón, but, a few minutes later, the latter's engine seized up, and he was forced to land violently off the field at Baulvok. The ensign landed between some buildings, in a clearing of about 100m, broke several posts and finally hit a railway carriage, which was knocked off the track. The consequences were a completely wrecked Fw 190, a German with a broken arm and a Spanish pilot … completely unhurt!

Several Spanish pilots of the 4th and 5th Squadrons consult a map during the adaptation period of the new arrivals in the USSR.

Somewhat later, Ensign Jesús Orúe Puga, who was point for Commander Cuadra, had his engine stop, but he was lucky and managed to land, with the train inside, on the bank of an icy river. He was also unharmed.

For his part, Lieutenant Eduardo Vega de Seoane Barroso took off with Lieutenant Valiente but returned immediately when he was unable to retract the landing gear of his Fw 190. It was clear that the start of the 5th Squadron's flights had turned out to be a disaster, but it was not the pilots who were to blame but rather the tremendous state of exhaustion suffered by the Fw 190s.

Then, the weather worsened again, and snow made its appearance, so flights were again disrupted for the whole week.

Finally, on 24 January, five Messerschmitt Bf 109 G-6s were received. The Germans put them in a hangar for an overhaul because, as with all the aircraft delivered to the Spanish, they were not new and had already served in the *Luftwaffe*. The first thing they did was remove the bomb launchers they carried.

On 25 January, the ground echelon arrived under the command of Lieutenant Antonio del Río Amado. The new arrivals watched in amazement as a group of Germans, whom the veterans called '*Los Funerarios*' (The Undertakers), set about placing bombs all over the buildings and installations, with the aim of blowing them up in the event of an attack.

Finally, on 5 February 1944, taking advantage of an improvement in the weather, several pilots took off to test the *Chichones*. Then, the weather worsened, and the fog rolled in, so flights were interrupted again.

Ensign Jesús Orúe Puga with a comrade from the 5th Squadron. This pilot arrived at Bobruisk on 9 January together with his comrades from the 1st Patrol: Captain Arróniz, Lieutenants Gil and Vega and Ensign Tassara.

The inspector commander of the 4th Squadron, Major Cuadra, sitting on the wing of a Bf 109 G-6 next to the inspector commander of the 5th Squadron, Major Murcia, during the relief of one squadron by the other. Both pilots had already demonstrated their expertise during the GCE.

Major Javier Murcia Rubio getting out of his Bf 109 G-6 after one of the few missions that the 5th Blue Squadron had the opportunity to carry out during the month it was deployed on the Eastern Front.

Several pilots and mechanics of the 5th Squadron pose on a horse-drawn sledge next to one of the Spanish unit's Bf 109 G-6s.

Several Spanish officers of the 5th Squadron during a relaxing moment, having a drink. The shield of the 4th Blue Squadron can still be seen on the wall in the background.

On 19 February and aboard the Ju 52 liaison aircraft, Major Javier Murcia, the 5th Squadron's inspector commander, arrived, as did the members of his second expedition: Captain Juan Carbó Amiguet, Lieutenants Francisco Sacanelles Cerveró, Jaime Maura Pieres, Antonio García Carretero and Estanislao Segurola Guereca and Ensign Pedro Santa Cruz Barceló.

As the weather improved again, the services increased, and Bf 109 G-6s began to engage Yak-9s in several combats, all without consequence.

Lieutenant Francisco Sacanelles Cerveró posing next to a Ju 52. The pilot's clothes show how cold it was at the base where the Spanish were deployed.

Captain Juan Carbó Amiguet of the 2nd Patrol of the 5th Blue Squadron during a break in the rear.

The cold appearance of the airfield where the Spanish unit was based is evident in this 'snowy' picture.

On 27 February, a Spanish patrol took off, consisting of four Bf 109 G-6 aircraft: Major Murcia and Lieutenant Carretero as his wingman and Lieutenant Segurola and Ensign Tassara as his wingman. Their mission was to escort a Ju 87 formation over the Paritschi area, which was carried out without incident. But, when the *Stukas* had already bombed, the second pair lost sight of the first, and then Lieutenant Segurola heard the base transmitter warn of the presence of enemy aircraft in low-level flight. When they were flying at Paritschi's height (4,500m), they saw two planes flying very low and dived for them. Ensign Tassara's radio was inoperative, and he lost sight of Lieutenant Segurola, hoping to see him again once they pulled up, but this did not happen. After a few minutes of searching, the ensign joined the first pair, and they returned to the Bobruisk camp. Once there, they were informed that a Bf 109 had been sighted going down south of the village of Moisejewka, south-east of Paritschi. The wreckage of the aircraft and its pilot were unrecognisable, but there was no doubt to the man's identity, as he was the only casualty suffered by the *Luftwaffe*. Lieutenant Segurola had gone down in his fourth war service in his Messerschmitt Bf 109 G-6 Werk N.411218. He was the only pilot of the 5th Blue Squadron to be shot down and the last Spanish pilot of all the Blue Squadrons to be shot down in Russia.

Major Javier Murcia, inspector commander of the 5th Squadron. Like the rest of the pilots in his unit, he failed to shoot down any enemy aircraft during the 5th Squadron's month of activity.

Ensign Tassara of the 1st Patrol of the 5th Blue Squadron. This pilot was the wingman for Lieutenant Estanislao Segurola when he crashed his Bf 109 G-6 on 27 February 1944.

Grave of Lieutenant Estanislao Segurola in Bobruisk. This pilot was the last of all the Blue Squadrons to be shot down in Russia.

That same day, Captain Isaac Arróniz Larios tried to reach the place where Segurola had crashed but was unable to do so until the following day. He found it about eight kilometres away, at the entrance to a forest. With some pieces of the propeller, they made a cross and put his name on it. His remains were collected and taken to the Bobruisk airfield, where he received the corresponding military honours.

The pilots of the 5th Squadron were only able to fly for a few more days – with neither any enemy shootdowns nor new casualties of their own – because, a few days later in Berlin, when the Spanish ambassador was presenting the new military attaché at the Reich Foreign Ministry, Lieutenant Colonel Ángel Salas Larrazabal, who was the commander of the 1st Blue Squadron, they were unexpectedly informed that the Spanish government had given the order to repatriate the squadron, as well as the Blue Legion (the official repatriation order had already existed since 6 March).

On 15 March, the Ju 52 liaison aircraft landed at Bobruisk, carrying an order for Major Murcia to report to Berlin. Upon his return three days later, he informed his men of the order to hand over the planes and their imminent return to Spain. The Spanish presence in the fight against the USSR was beginning to come to an end.

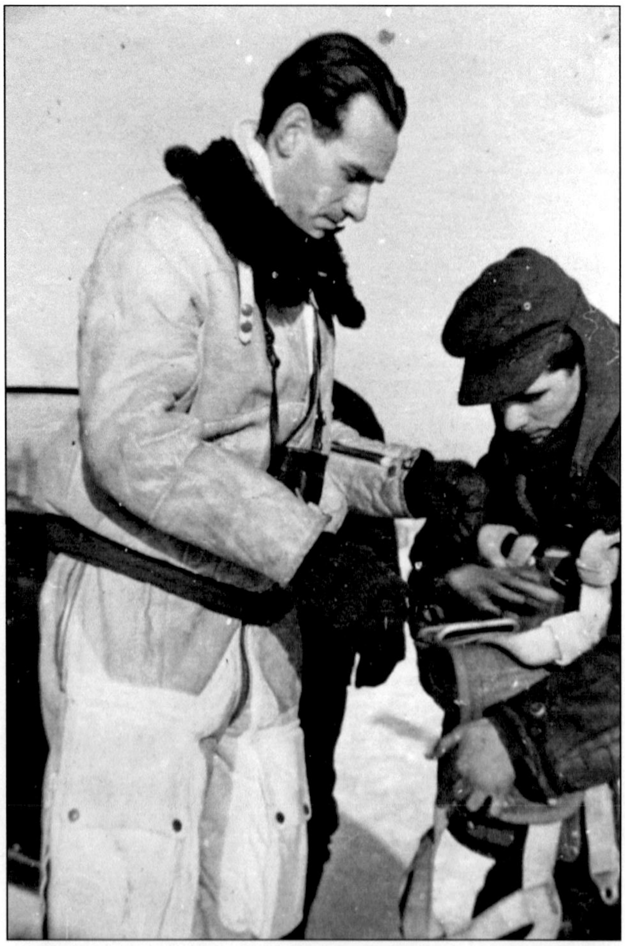

Captain Isaac Arróniz of the 5th Squadron being helped by a mechanic with his parachute to get ready for his next flight.

Two mechanics next to one of the Bf 109 G-6s of the 5th Squadron. This unit was the only one of the Spanish squadrons that did not manage to shoot down any enemy aircraft, partly due to the short time it spent on the front.

Lieutenant Cruzate, pilot of the Spanish Ju 52 that transported the pilots of the 1st Patrol of the 5th Squadron to Bobruisk after a few days in Berlin.

On 18 March, the 5th Squadron (1st and 2nd Patrols) was ordered to hand over its Bf 109 G-6 aircraft. The official farewell of the 5th Blue Squadron was given by the commander of *1. Flieger-Division*, Robert Fuchs. The feeling was similar to that of the soldiers of the Blue Division and Blue Legion: they were being forced to abandon their German comrades when the war was becoming more difficult for the Axis. The Spaniards began to prepare all the material for their return to Spain, and, on 26 March, after a farewell breakfast with *Kommodore* Nordmann and their German comrades of JG 51, Major Murcia and his pilots left in the Ju 52 liaison plane for Spain. The last men belonging to the ground echelon crossed the border between France and Spain on 22 April. The 5th Squadron had almost a month's operational period within the *Luftwaffe*, so it barely had the time to carry out an adequate number of missions. Of course, the return to Spain was completely hushed up by the Spanish government, which did not want further trouble with the Allies.

Members of the 5th Squadron with the Ju 52 liaison at the Bobruisk airfield on 26 March 1944. The repatriation of the 5th Squadron took place even before the entire unit was assembled on Soviet soil. Among the men in the picture is Major Murcia on the left wearing a peaked cap.

Nordmann and Murcia shake hands during the farewell ceremony for the Spanish unit. Although a 6th Blue Squadron was planned, it never had the chance to be created.

Major Murcia (on the left with the Spanish coat of arms on his right arm) and *Oberstleutnant* Nordmann, *Kommodore* of JG 51, during the farewell ceremony of the 5th Squadron at the Bobruisk airfield on 26 March 1944.

The pilots of the 5th Blue Squadron flew 86 missions and participated in six engagements. It did not reach full strength, nor did it claim any shootdowns. However, it had to bear the loss of one pilot (the shootdown occurred when it was still the 4th Blue Squadron flying in Russia, although with pilots from the 5th Squadron attached) and two Bf 109 G-6s, although one was not due to the enemy.

The Russian adventure had just ended. The Spaniards had remained there from 1 October 1941 to 26 March 1944, practically two-and-a-half years in which they had managed to shoot down 168 aircraft in 4,944 war services and 611 engagements, suffering 24 casualties between the dead and missing.

The Spanish government rewarded them with 16 Individual Military Medals (*Medallas Militares Individuales*), 38 War Crosses with Palms and 27 promotions on the scale for war merits. For its part, the German government awarded a German Cross in Gold (to Major Ángel Salas), 74 Iron Crosses 2nd and 1st Class, 65 gold, silver and bronze pins for outstanding merits in flight and 571 War Merit Crosses with Swords.

Three mechanics pose for a souvenir photograph next to one of the 5th Squadron's Bf 109 G-6s in winter camouflage.

The Ju 52 liaison used by the Spanish units after suffering an accident that caused the port landing gear to break.

Appendices

Air Victories of the Blue Squadrons

The five Blue Squadrons remained on the front lines for almost 30 months, from October 1941 to March 1944. During these months, they flew 4,944 combat missions, with 611 engagements against the enemy, and managed to shoot down 164 Soviet aircraft. On the negative side, the Spanish squadrons had 19 pilot officers KIA or MIA, one pilot taken prisoner, four dead from the ground echelon and several wounded of varying severity.

Many of its pilots and ground echelon personnel received Spanish and German decorations in recognition of their bravery and courage during the months they fought in Russia.

Among the Spanish pilots, there were 13 aces (i.e., pilots who shot down at least five enemy aircraft each), although the small period of time in which each of the five Blue Squadrons fought in Russia meant that the number of aircraft shot down by Spanish pilots was not as high as that of their German comrades. It is also necessary to remember not only that several pilots had flown during the GCE and had achieved shootdowns before going to Russia but also that most of the pilots had no previous combat experience. The most outstanding pilots were Captain Hevia (3rd Squadron, 12 downs), Major Cuadra (4th Squadron, 10 downs), Lieutenant Sánchez-Arjona (4th Squadron, nine downs) and Captain Gavilán (3rd Squadron, nine downs).

It is also important to remember that, although apparently the number of shootdowns was not very high (in comparison to Axis countries such as Romania, Italy, Bulgaria or Finland), the Blue Squadrons were organised according to the principle of pilot rotation. For this reason, the periods of combat service were only several months, which, together with the bad weather that often prevailed in the USSR, meant that the Spaniards had fewer opportunities to achieve shootdowns in the first place.

One fact to note is that the Germans consented to lend their aircraft to pilots belonging to a country that was not at war.[1] Also, as mentioned above, the Germans really appreciated and respected the Spanish pilots for their bravery and virtuosity in flying, having fought shoulder to shoulder with them during the GCE. The following list of the shootdowns achieved by the pilots of the different Blue Squadrons is based on the work of Juan Arráez Cerdá:[2]

1 Caballero and Guillén, *Escuadrillas azules en Rusia*, pp.18–20.

2 Arráez Cerdá, 'Les Espagnols de la Luftwaffe', 18, pp.26, 52, 76 and 'Les Espagnols de la Luftwaffe', 19, pp.28, 37.

Shootdowns Achieved by the Blue Squadron Pilots

Rank	Pilot	Blue Squadron	GCE Aircraft Shootdowns	USSR Aircraft Shootdowns	Notes
Captain	Hevia Álvarez de Quiñones	3rd	–	12	
Major	Cuadra Medina	4th	–	10	
Captain	Gavilán Ponce de León	3rd	–	9	
Lieutenant	Sánchez-Arjona Courtoy	4th	–	9	Killed on 19 November 1943
Ensign	Aldecoa Lecanda	3rd/4th	–	7	
Lieutenant	Arango López	4th	–	7	
Major	Salas Larrazabal	1st	16 1/3	6	Two on land
Lieutenant	Azqueta Brunet	3rd	–	6	
Lieutenant	Sánchez-Tabernero de Prada	4th	–	6	
Lieutenant	Valiente Zárraga	4th	–	6	
Lieutenant	Lucas Fernández-Peña	4th	–	6	
Captain	Alós Herreros	3rd	–	5	
Captain	Bengoechea Menchaca	2nd	–	4 (1 probable)	
Lieutenant	Meneses Orozco	3rd/4th	–	6	Two with the 4th Squadron
Lieutenant	Barañano Martínez	2nd/3rd	–	4	Two with the 3rd Squadron
Ensign	Mateos Recio	4th	–	4	
Lieutenant	Pérez Muñoz	3rd	–	4	
Lieutenant	Martínez Vara de Rey	3rd	–	4	
Captain	Llaca Álvarez	4th	–	4	
Lieutenant	Cavanilles Vereterra	4th	–	4	Missing on 10 January 1944
Major	Ferrándiz Arjonilla	3rd	–	3	
Lieutenant	Calleja González-Camino	3rd	–	3	
Captain	Bayo Alesandri	1st	11	3	One on land
Captain	De Frutos Rubio	2nd	2	2	
Ensign	Beriaín Arbilla	2nd/3rd	–	2	
Ensign	Guibert Love	3rd/4th	–	2	One with the 4th Squadron
Lieutenant	Escalante de la Lastra	4th	–	2	
Ensign	Chicharro Lamamie de Clairac	4th	–	1	Killed on 21 August 1943
Lieutenant	Ibarreche Arriaga	1st	7	1	
Captain	Serra Pablo-Romero	2nd	3 1/3	1	
Lieutenant	Garret Rueda	2nd/3rd	–	1	
Lieutenant	Pérez González	3rd	–	1	Killed on 8 June 1943
Lieutenant	Escudé Gisbert	2nd	–	1	
Lieutenant	Arango López	2nd	–	1	
Lieutenant	Arraiza Goñi	2nd	–	1	
Lieutenant	Medrano de Pedro	2nd	–	1	
Ensign	Bengoa Cremades	2nd/3rd	–	1	
Lieutenant	Luca de Tena y Laso	3rd	1	1	
Lieutenant	Lacruz Cuervo	3rd	–	1	
Lieutenant	Roselló Simonet	3rd	–	1	Killed on 5 May 1943
Lieutenant	Serra Alorda	4th	4	1	
Lieutenant	Zorita Alonso	1st	–	–	One on land

Table 3 is a comprehensive breakdown of each of the Blue Squadrons, also according to Arráez Cerdá's work.[3]

The Blue Squadrons

	1st Expeditionary Squadron	**2nd Expeditionary Squadron**	**3rd Expeditionary Squadron**	**4th Expeditionary Squadron**	**5th Expeditionary Squadron**
Designation in the *Luftwaffe*	15.(Span)/JG 27 *VIII. Fliegerkorps*, *Luftflotte* 2	15.(Span)/JG 51 *Luftwaffen-kommando Ost*	15.(Span)/JG 51 *Luftwaffen-kommando Ost*	15.(Span)/JG 51 *1. Flieger-Division*, *Luftflotte* 6	15.(Span)/JG 51 *1. Flieger-Division*, *Luftflotte* 6
Incorporated	14 July 1941	6 February 1942	17 September 1942	2 April 1943	26 October 1943
Arrival at the Front	1 October 1941	8 June 1942	1 December 1942	4 July 1943	10 January 1944
Operational Bases	Moschna 24.9.1941–7.10.1941 Bjeloj 7.10.1941–9.10.1941 Konaja 9.10.1941–16.10.1941 Kalinin 16.10.1941–28.10.1941 Staritza 28.10.1941–6.11.1941 Russa 6.11.1941–25.11.1941 Klin 25.11.1941–10.12.1941 Russa 10.12.1941–15.12.1941 Dugvino 15.12.1941–7.1.1942 Vitebsk 7.1.1942–13.2.1942	Orel-West	Orel Seschtschinskaja (2 patrols) Smolensk (1 patrol)	Seschtschinskaja (1 patrol) Bryansk (1 patrol) Vitebsk (1 patrol) Smolensk-North Orsha Stara Bychow Bobruisk	Bobruisk
Withdrawal from the Front	2 February 1942	30 November 1942	30 June 1943	23 February 1944	26 March 1944
Dissolved	4 March 1942	23 December 1942		22 April 1944	
Aircraft Used	Bf 109 E-7/B	Bf 109 F-2	Bf 109 F-2 Bf 109 F-4 Fw 190 A-2 Fw 190 A-3	Fw 190 A-2 Fw 190 A-3 Bf 109 G-6	Bf 109 G-6
Missions Undertaken	460	1,312	1,716	1,918	86
Air Combat	94	117	112	277	6
Shootdowns	10 (+ 4 on land)	13	62 (+ 1 Hevia in a German *Staffel*)	74	0
Enemy Aircraft Types	3 Pe-2 1 I-16 1 I-18 (MiG-3?) 1 DB-3 1 Pe-3	6 LaGG-3 3 Il-2 3 Pe-2 1 DB-3	26 LaGG-3 6 A-5 3 Yak-1 1 I-153 10 Pe-2 15 Il-2	26 LaGG-3 22 La-5 1 Yak-9 19 Il-2 several more unspecified	0
Pilots[4]	17 (5)	19 (2)	19 (5)	20 (7)	14 (1)
Ground Staff[5]	93 (1)	100 (1)	107 (1)	132 (0)	117 (0)

	Aircraft Shot Down + Destroyed on the Ground	**Pilots**	**Casualties**
Total	159 + 4 + 1	90	25

3 Arráez Cerdá, 'Les Espagnols de la Luftwaffe', 18, pp.26, 52, 76 and 'Les Espagnols de la Luftwaffe', 19, pp.28, 37.
4 Number of casualties in parentheses.
5 Number of casualties in parentheses.

Another very important aspect to bear in mind is the type of opponent the Spanish pilots encountered in the skies over the USSR. At the beginning of the German invasion of the USSR, the Soviet pilots were not at the same level as the *Luftwaffe* pilots. This fact gradually changed during the war, and, from 1943 onwards, the performance of Soviet pilots in air combat was much better. To this must be added the aircraft that the Soviets used for the most part until 1942–1943 and from that moment onwards, as they went from obsolete aircraft such as the I-153, I-16 and LaGG-3 to aircraft with higher performance (which became superior to German aircraft when the Soviet pilots got the right performance out of them) such as the LaGG-5, La-5 and Yak-9. The Spanish pilots of the Blue Squadrons were able to experience these changes in Soviet air power between 1941 and 1944 and witness how it became increasingly difficult to shoot down enemy aircraft. Nevertheless, the pilots of the 3rd and 4th Blue Squadrons managed to shoot down many Soviet aircraft, as the possibility of confrontation with the Soviets increased greatly during 1943.

So far, we have recounted many of the air victories of Spanish pilots, although not all of them. And we have shown how the greatest number of air clashes between the Spanish and the Soviets were with fighters, second greatest with attack aircraft (such as the Il-2) and, in a smaller number of cases, with bombers.

Based on the excellent work by Arráez Cerdá, Table 4 shows the types of aircraft shot down by the different Blue Squadrons.[6]

Types of Aircraft Shot Down by the Blue Squadrons

	1st Squadron	2nd Squadron	3rd Squadron	4th Squadron	5th Squadron	Total Shootdowns
I-16	1					1
I-18	2 (+ 2 on land)					2 (+ 2)
DB-3	5	1				6
Pe-2	1	3	10 (+ 1 Hevia)	2		16 (+ 1)
LaGG-3		6	26	26		58
Il-2		3	15	19		37
LaGG-5/La-5			6	22		28
Yak-1			3	1		4
I-153			1			1
Boston				3		3
Balloon				1		1
Other	1 (+ 2 on land)		1			2 (+ 2)

The worth of the Spanish pilots who made up the various Blue Squadrons is endorsed by the citation even in one of the orders of the day corresponding to JG 51 when celebrating 6,000 aerial victories: ‘For more than a year now our Spanish comrades have been at our side, animated by a tireless will to fight, overcoming all the numerous difficulties presented in their path and have contributed to help JG 51, with all enthusiasm, achieving the successes of which we are so proud’.[7]

As we have described in this text, and according to Carlos Caballero, the brave behaviour of the soldiers belonging to the different Blue Squadrons allowed these Spaniards to be awarded a German Gold Cross, 74 Iron Crosses 2nd and 1st Class, 571 War Merit Crosses and 65 gold, silver and bronze flight pins by the German Reich.[8]

In Spain, the men of the Blue Squadrons received several Individual Military Merit Medals, 38 War Crosses with Palms and 27 promotions. But much more important was the military career of many of them, which allowed them to reach high positions within the Spanish Army. The commander of the 1st Squadron, Ángel Salas, became captain general, and several of the pilots reached the rank of lieutenant general or general. These men also became the elite of Spanish pilots after the Second World War, although that belongs to another era that will not be dealt with in this text.

6 Arráez Cerdá, ‘Les Espagnols de la Luftwaffe’, 18, pp.26, 52, 76 and ‘Les Espagnols de la Luftwaffe’, 19, pp.28, 37.
7 Caballero and Guillén, *Escuadrillas azules en Rusia*, p.86.
8 Caballero and Guillén, *Escuadrillas azules en Rusia*, pp.98–108.

Ranks and Equivalences of the Spanish Air Force

Due to the presence of Spanish pilots in the Blue Squadrons, we consider it important to recall in this Appendix the equivalences between the ranks of the EdA and the *Luftwaffe*.

EdA Ranks in the *Luftwaffe*

EdA Rank	English Translation	*Luftwaffe* Equivalent
Capitán General	Captain General	*Generalfeldmarschall*
General del Aire	Air General	*Generaloberst*
Teniente General	Lieutenant General	*General der Luftwaffe*
General de División	Major General	*Generalleutnant*
General de Brigada	Brigadier General	*Generalmajor*
Coronel	Colonel	*Oberst*
Teniente Coronel	Lieutenant Colonel	*Oberstleutnant*
Comandante	Major	*Major*
Capitán	Captain	*Hauptmann*
Teniente	Lieutenant	*Oberleutnant*
Suboficial Mayor	Ensign	*Leutnant*
Subteniente	Senior Non-Commissioned Officer	*Stabsfeldwebel*
Brigada	Second Lieutenant	*Oberfeldwebel*
Sargento	Brigadier	*Feldwebel*
Cabo 1º	Sergeant	*Unteroffizier*
Suboficial Mayor	Lance Corporal	*Obergefreiter*
Subteniente	Corporal	*Gefreiter*
Brigada	Soldier	*Flieger*

Emblems

The Blue Squadron aircraft used the same insignia as the *Luftwaffe* aircraft: the swastika, or *Hakenkreuz*, on the tail and the *Balkenkreuz* on the fuselage and wings. The Spanish aircraft also used the theatre of operations markings, which consisted of yellow paint on the nose and wingtips of the aircraft in addition to the yellow stripe on the fuselage. The Spanish Ju 52s used on the Eastern Front wore German insignia as well. The only significant difference from the other *Luftwaffe* aircraft on the Eastern Front was the insignia of the individual Blue Squadrons on the nose of the Spaniards' aircraft, although this insignia was not used on all of them.

Despite belonging to JG 27 and JG 51, we have not seen any photographs where the emblems of either JG can be seen on the Spanish aircraft. The insignia that was the symbol of the five Blue Squadrons was the insignia of Joaquín García Morato's fighter group, leader of the national fighter aviation during the GCE. But each squadron made some modifications, so there were five different insignia that were used by the Blue Squadrons.

On the nose of the Bf 109 Es of the 1st Squadron, the mechanics painted the insignia of Joaquín García Morato's fighter group accompanied by a Roman numeral two (II). This II indicated that this was the second fight of the members of the famous unit against communism, as they had fought previously during the GCE. There are photographs showing the use of this emblem.

On the Bf 109 Es of the 2nd Squadron, the emblem of Joaquín García Morato's fighter group was maintained, although on a red St James' Cross. Apostle Santiago is the patron saint of Spain, so it was decided to use his cross. There are photographs showing the use of this emblem.

The 3rd Squadron again used the emblem of Joaquín García Morato's fighter group, although on a German cross, or *Balkenkreuz* (the same as that used by the *Luftwaffe* aircraft). The situation of the Second World War and the changes in the aircraft used by the Spanish pilots meant that this emblem was ultimately not used on the nose of the fighters.

In the 4th Squadron, Joaquín García Morato's ubiquitous fighter group emblem was placed over the German fighter emblem (a winged arrow surrounded by a wreath of laurels). As with the 3rd Squadron, in the end, this emblem was not used on the nose of the fighters.

The 5th Blue Squadron, despite its brief period of action on the Eastern Front, also had its own emblem. Similar to that of the 1st Squadron, the insignia of Joaquín García Morato's fighter group was accompanied by a Roman numeral five (V) replacing the II.

The emblem of Joaquín García Morato's squadron was a white circle with three birds in the centre (a falcon, bustard and blackbird) and the phrase '*Vista, suerte, y al toro*' (Sight, luck, and the bull). The falcon represented García Morato, the bustard represented Bermúdez de Castro, and the blackbird represented Julio Salvador – the three founders of the Morato fighter group. The phrase that served as the motto for the unit was and is used by bullfighters when entering the bullring to face the uncertainty of their fate. They never know if they will get out of there alive. Everything depends on their eyesight, their luck and their determination. The pilots obviously thought that, in their aerial combats, they would need eyesight, luck and determination.

Aircraft Used by the Expeditionary Squadrons

The Spanish expeditionary squadrons had the opportunity to use different models of aircraft while fighting in the skies over Russia. There were four aircraft models: the Messerschmitt Bf 109 E-7 (E-4), Messerschmitt Bf 109 F-4, Focke-Wulf Fw 190 A-3 and Messerschmitt Bf 109 G-6. All aircraft were the same as those used by other *Luftwaffe* units, although it is true that, when the Spanish used the E model, some *Luftwaffe* units were already using the F and that, when the Spanish used the F, some German units were already using the Fw 190.

Messerschmitt Bf 109 E-7

The Spanish pilots of the 1st Squadron were able to adapt more easily to the E-7 model of the Bf 109, as it had already been used in Spain during the GCE. In addition, the EdA had several Bf 109 E-1s and E-3s, so there were several pilot officers who were already familiar with the use of the aircraft.

With the Messerschmitt, the Spaniards had an aircraft that could perform both fighter or escort and ground attack missions.

The E-7 was a 'long-range' version of the E-4 (itself a version of the E-3 with improved armament of Oerlikon MG-FF/M guns on each wing and a higher rate of fire), capable of mounting a 300l external tank.

Messerschmitt Bf 109 F-4

The F-4 was possibly the best Bf 109 of all the models produced in terms of performance and firepower (later models increased in weight with new engines and weapons systems, decreasing its manoeuvrability). It was the most widely used version of the F series.

This model of the Bf 109 was used by the Spanish as a pure fighter, which was the mission for which it was built.

Focke-Wulf Fw 190 A-3

The 4th Blue Squadron had the opportunity to use powerful German aircraft. The Fw 190 was characterised by its great manoeuvrability, high top speed, great structural robustness, very powerful armament and a plexiglass cockpit that allowed great visibility. Its four cannons and two machine guns had a devastating effect on enemy aircraft – something the Spanish were quick to see. The change from the F-model Bf 109 to the Fw 190 was very important for the Spanish pilots, as they were able to fly a completely different aircraft to the Messerschmitt and one that the EdA did not have, thus allowing the Spaniards to increase their training.

Messerschmitt Bf 109 G-6

The G-6 model of the Bf 109 was the result of Germany's need for faster aircraft to cope with enemy aircraft. The increased power and speed in the fuselage of the Bf 109 resulted in the aircraft being heavier and having reduced manoeuvrability in order to gain speed and horizontal acceleration. It was the most heavily built version of the Bf 109 and was intended as an armament platform, as field modifications (*Rüstsätse*) could be installed at airfields on the front line.

Aircraft Used by the Blue Squadrons

Model	Squadron	Armament	Motor
Messerschmitt Bf 109 E-7	1st	2 cannons (20mm) + 2 machine guns (7.92mm)	Daimler-Benz DB 601 A (1,175 hp)
Messerschmitt Bf 109 F-4	2nd and 3rd	1 cannon (20mm) + 2 machine guns (7.92mm)	Daimler-Benz DB 601 E (1,350 hp)
Focke-Wulf Fw 190 A-3	4th	4 cannons (20mm) + 2 machine guns (7.92mm)	BMW 801 D-2 (1,700 hp)
Messerschmitt Bf 109 G-6	5th	1 cannon (30mm) + 2 machine guns (13mm)	Daimler-Benz DB 605 A (1,475 hp)

Bibliography

Primary Sources

Arráez Cerdá, Juan, 'Les Espagnols de la Luftwaffe: Les Escadrilles Bleues', *Ciel de Guerre*, 18 (2010), pp.3–76
Arráez Cerdá, Juan, 'Les Espagnols de la Luftwaffe: Les Escadrilles Bleues', *Ciel de Guerre*, 19 (2011), pp.3–82
Caballero, Carlos, and Guillén, Santiago, *Escuadrillas azules en Rusia: Historia y uniformes* (Madrid: Almena, 1999)
Caballero Jurado, Carlos, *Spaniards in the Luftwaffe: Blue Squadron in Russia* (Madrid: Tikal, 2014)
Fernández-Coppel Larrinaga, Jorge, *The Blue Squadron* (Madrid: La Esfera de los Libros, 2006)
Gil Martínez, Eduardo M., *Fuerza Aérea Española durante la 2ª Guerra Mundial* (Madrid: Almena, 2019)
Gil Martínez, Eduardo M., *Spanish Air Force during World War II: Germany's Hidden Ally?* (Świdnik: Kagero, 2019)
Martínez Canales, Francisco, *Spanish Wings in Russia 1941/44: Blue Squadrons in the Luftwaffe* (Madrid: Almena, 2011)

Secondary Sources

Angelucci, Enzo, Matricardi, Paolo, and Pinto, Pierluigi, *Complete book of World War II Combat Aircraft* (Vercelli: White Star Publishers, 2001)
Arias Ramos, Raúl, *Legión Cóndor: Su historia 60 años después* (Madrid: Almena, 2000)
Bueno Carrera, José María, *The Blue Division and Squadron: Its Organisation and Uniforms* (Madrid: Aldaba, 2003)
Gil Martínez, Eduardo M., *The Spanish in the SS and Wehrmacht, 1944-1945: The Ezquerra Unit in the Battle of Berlin* (Atglen, PA: Schiffer Publishing, 2012)
Ministerio de Defensa, *Aviones militares españoles* (Madrid: Ministerio de Defensa, 1986)
Neulen, Hans Werner, *In the Skies of Europe: Air Forces Allied to the Luftwaffe 1939–1945* (Ramsbury: The Crowood Press, 2000)
Weal, John, *Jagdgeschwader 27 'Afrika'* (Oxford: Osprey Publishing, 2003)
Weal, John, *Jagdgeschwader 51 'Mölders'* (Oxford: Osprey Publishing, 2006)